# Telephone Book

1  Pick-up the telephone
2  Say Good Morning or Good Afternoon
3  State your name and the name of your company
4  State your name
5  Ask how you can help
6  Listen to the caller
7  Note the callers, name, telephone number and the message
8  Update Producteev
9  Bill the call to the relevant client

Copyright © 2017

First Published in Great Britain in 2017 by Julie C Farmer.
The right of Julie Farmer to be identified as the Author of the work has been asserted by him in accordance with the Copyright, Designs and Patent Act 1988.

ISBN-13: 978-1530942336

Publishers Address
Brunel House, Volunteer Way, Faringdon, SN7 7YR

Telephone Numbers used daily

| Name | Phone | Company | Name | Phone | Company |
|------|-------|---------|------|-------|---------|
|      |       |         |      |       |         |
|      |       |         |      |       |         |
|      |       |         |      |       |         |
|      |       |         |      |       |         |
|      |       |         |      |       |         |
|      |       |         |      |       |         |
|      |       |         |      |       |         |
|      |       |         |      |       |         |
|      |       |         |      |       |         |
|      |       |         |      |       |         |
|      |       |         |      |       |         |
|      |       |         |      |       |         |
|      |       |         |      |       |         |
|      |       |         |      |       |         |
|      |       |         |      |       |         |
|      |       |         |      |       |         |
|      |       |         |      |       |         |
|      |       |         |      |       |         |
|      |       |         |      |       |         |
|      |       |         |      |       |         |
|      |       |         |      |       |         |

| Date | Details | | Billing | Person |
|---|---|---|---|---|
| ___/___/___ | Client: | | | |
| | | | Tel No | |
| | | | | |
| | | | | |
| | | | | |

| No Action | | Emailed | | Call Forward | | Client Task | | Update Producteev | |
|---|---|---|---|---|---|---|---|---|---|

| Date | Details | | Billing | Person |
|---|---|---|---|---|
| ___/___/___ | Client: | | | |
| | | | Tel No | |
| | | | | |
| | | | | |
| | | | | |

| No Action | | Emailed | | Call Forward | | Client Task | | Update Producteev | |
|---|---|---|---|---|---|---|---|---|---|

| Date | Details | | Billing | Person |
|---|---|---|---|---|
| ___/___/___ | Client: | | | |
| | | | Tel No | |
| | | | | |
| | | | | |
| | | | | |

| No Action | | Emailed | | Call Forward | | Client Task | | Update Producteev | |
|---|---|---|---|---|---|---|---|---|---|

| Date | Details | | Billing | Person |
|---|---|---|---|---|
| ___/___/___ | Client: | | | |
| | | | Tel No | |
| | | | | |
| | | | | |
| | | | | |

| No Action | | Emailed | | Call Forward | | Client Task | | Update Producteev | |
|---|---|---|---|---|---|---|---|---|---|

| Date | Details | | Billing | Person |
|---|---|---|---|---|
| ___/___/___ | Client: | | | |
| | | | Tel No | |
| | _____ | | | |
| | _____ | | | |

| No Action | | Emailed | | Call Forward | | Client Task | | Update Producteev | |
|---|---|---|---|---|---|---|---|---|---|

| Date | Details | | Billing | Person |
|---|---|---|---|---|
| ___/___/___ | Client: | | | |
| | | | Tel No | |
| | _____ | | | |
| | _____ | | | |

| No Action | | Emailed | | Call Forward | | Client Task | | Update Producteev | |
|---|---|---|---|---|---|---|---|---|---|

| Date | Details | | Billing | Person |
|---|---|---|---|---|
| ___/___/___ | Client: | | | |
| | | | Tel No | |
| | _____ | | | |
| | _____ | | | |

| No Action | | Emailed | | Call Forward | | Client Task | | Update Producteev | |
|---|---|---|---|---|---|---|---|---|---|

| Date | Details | | Billing | Person |
|---|---|---|---|---|
| ___/___/___ | Client: | | | |
| | | | Tel No | |
| | _____ | | | |
| | _____ | | | |

| No Action | | Emailed | | Call Forward | | Client Task | | Update Producteev | |
|---|---|---|---|---|---|---|---|---|---|

| Date | Details | | Billing | Person |
|---|---|---|---|---|
| ___/___/___ | Client: | | | |
| | | | Tel No | |
| | | | | |
| No Action | | Emailed | | Call Forward | | Client Task | | Update Producteev | |

| Date | Details | | Billing | Person |
|---|---|---|---|---|
| ___/___/___ | Client: | | | |
| | | | Tel No | |
| | | | | |
| No Action | | Emailed | | Call Forward | | Client Task | | Update Producteev | |

| Date | Details | | Billing | Person |
|---|---|---|---|---|
| ___/___/___ | Client: | | | |
| | | | Tel No | |
| | | | | |
| No Action | | Emailed | | Call Forward | | Client Task | | Update Producteev | |

| Date | Details | | Billing | Person |
|---|---|---|---|---|
| ___/___/___ | Client: | | | |
| | | | Tel No | |
| | | | | |
| No Action | | Emailed | | Call Forward | | Client Task | | Update Producteev | |

| Date | Details | | Billing | Person |
|---|---|---|---|---|
| __/__/__ | Client: | | | |
| | | | Tel No | |
| | | | | |
| No Action | | Emailed | | Call Forward | | Client Task | | Update Producteev | |

| Date | Details | | Billing | Person |
|---|---|---|---|---|
| __/__/__ | Client: | | | |
| | | | Tel No | |
| | | | | |
| No Action | | Emailed | | Call Forward | | Client Task | | Update Producteev | |

| Date | Details | | Billing | Person |
|---|---|---|---|---|
| __/__/__ | Client: | | | |
| | | | Tel No | |
| | | | | |
| No Action | | Emailed | | Call Forward | | Client Task | | Update Producteev | |

| Date | Details | | Billing | Person |
|---|---|---|---|---|
| __/__/__ | Client: | | | |
| | | | Tel No | |
| | | | | |
| No Action | | Emailed | | Call Forward | | Client Task | | Update Producteev | |

| Date | Details | | Billing | Person |
|---|---|---|---|---|
| ___/___/___ | Client: | | | |
| | | | Tel No | |
| | | | | |
| | | | | |
| | | | | |

| No Action | | Emailed | | Call Forward | | Client Task | | Update Producteev | |
|---|---|---|---|---|---|---|---|---|---|

| Date | Details | | Billing | Person |
|---|---|---|---|---|
| ___/___/___ | Client: | | | |
| | | | Tel No | |
| | | | | |
| | | | | |
| | | | | |

| No Action | | Emailed | | Call Forward | | Client Task | | Update Producteev | |
|---|---|---|---|---|---|---|---|---|---|

| Date | Details | | Billing | Person |
|---|---|---|---|---|
| ___/___/___ | Client: | | | |
| | | | Tel No | |
| | | | | |
| | | | | |
| | | | | |

| No Action | | Emailed | | Call Forward | | Client Task | | Update Producteev | |
|---|---|---|---|---|---|---|---|---|---|

| Date | Details | | Billing | Person |
|---|---|---|---|---|
| ___/___/___ | Client: | | | |
| | | | Tel No | |
| | | | | |
| | | | | |
| | | | | |

| No Action | | Emailed | | Call Forward | | Client Task | | Update Producteev | |
|---|---|---|---|---|---|---|---|---|---|

| Date | Details | | Billing | Person |
|---|---|---|---|---|
| __/__/__ | Client: | | | |
| | | | Tel No | |
| | | | | |
| No Action | | Emailed | Call Forward | Client Task | Update Producteev |

| Date | Details | | Billing | Person |
|---|---|---|---|---|
| __/__/__ | Client: | | | |
| | | | Tel No | |
| | | | | |
| No Action | | Emailed | Call Forward | Client Task | Update Producteev |

| Date | Details | | Billing | Person |
|---|---|---|---|---|
| __/__/__ | Client: | | | |
| | | | Tel No | |
| | | | | |
| No Action | | Emailed | Call Forward | Client Task | Update Producteev |

| Date | Details | | Billing | Person |
|---|---|---|---|---|
| __/__/__ | Client: | | | |
| | | | Tel No | |
| | | | | |
| No Action | | Emailed | Call Forward | Client Task | Update Producteev |

| Date | Details | | Billing | Person |
|---|---|---|---|---|
| ___/___/___ | Client: | | | |
| | | | Tel No | |
| | _____ | | | |
| | _____ | | | |
| No Action | | Emailed | | Call Forward | | Client Task | | Update Producteev | |

| Date | Details | | Billing | Person |
|---|---|---|---|---|
| ___/___/___ | Client: | | | |
| | | | Tel No | |
| | _____ | | | |
| | _____ | | | |
| No Action | | Emailed | | Call Forward | | Client Task | | Update Producteev | |

| Date | Details | | Billing | Person |
|---|---|---|---|---|
| ___/___/___ | Client: | | | |
| | | | Tel No | |
| | _____ | | | |
| | _____ | | | |
| No Action | | Emailed | | Call Forward | | Client Task | | Update Producteev | |

| Date | Details | | Billing | Person |
|---|---|---|---|---|
| ___/___/___ | Client: | | | |
| | | | Tel No | |
| | _____ | | | |
| | _____ | | | |
| No Action | | Emailed | | Call Forward | | Client Task | | Update Producteev | |

| Date | Details | | Billing | Person |
|---|---|---|---|---|
| ___/___/___ | Client: | | | |
| | | | Tel No | |
| | | | | |

| No Action | | Emailed | | Call Forward | | Client Task | | Update Producteev | |
|---|---|---|---|---|---|---|---|---|---|

| Date | Details | | Billing | Person |
|---|---|---|---|---|
| ___/___/___ | Client: | | | |
| | | | Tel No | |
| | | | | |

| No Action | | Emailed | | Call Forward | | Client Task | | Update Producteev | |
|---|---|---|---|---|---|---|---|---|---|

| Date | Details | | Billing | Person |
|---|---|---|---|---|
| ___/___/___ | Client: | | | |
| | | | Tel No | |
| | | | | |

| No Action | | Emailed | | Call Forward | | Client Task | | Update Producteev | |
|---|---|---|---|---|---|---|---|---|---|

| Date | Details | | Billing | Person |
|---|---|---|---|---|
| ___/___/___ | Client: | | | |
| | | | Tel No | |
| | | | | |

| No Action | | Emailed | | Call Forward | | Client Task | | Update Producteev | |
|---|---|---|---|---|---|---|---|---|---|

| Date | Details | | Billing | Person |
|---|---|---|---|---|
| __/__/__ | Client: | | | |
| | | | Tel No | |
| | | | | |
| No Action | | Emailed | | Call Forward | | Client Task | | Update Producteev | |

| Date | Details | | Billing | Person |
|---|---|---|---|---|
| __/__/__ | Client: | | | |
| | | | Tel No | |
| | | | | |
| No Action | | Emailed | | Call Forward | | Client Task | | Update Producteev | |

| Date | Details | | Billing | Person |
|---|---|---|---|---|
| __/__/__ | Client: | | | |
| | | | Tel No | |
| | | | | |
| No Action | | Emailed | | Call Forward | | Client Task | | Update Producteev | |

| Date | Details | | Billing | Person |
|---|---|---|---|---|
| __/__/__ | Client: | | | |
| | | | Tel No | |
| | | | | |
| No Action | | Emailed | | Call Forward | | Client Task | | Update Producteev | |

| Date | Details | | Billing | Person |
|---|---|---|---|---|
| ___/___/___ | Client: | | | |
| | | | Tel No | |
| | | | | |

| No Action | | Emailed | | Call Forward | | Client Task | | Update Producteev | |
|---|---|---|---|---|---|---|---|---|---|

| Date | Details | | Billing | Person |
|---|---|---|---|---|
| ___/___/___ | Client: | | | |
| | | | Tel No | |
| | | | | |

| No Action | | Emailed | | Call Forward | | Client Task | | Update Producteev | |
|---|---|---|---|---|---|---|---|---|---|

| Date | Details | | Billing | Person |
|---|---|---|---|---|
| ___/___/___ | Client: | | | |
| | | | Tel No | |
| | | | | |

| No Action | | Emailed | | Call Forward | | Client Task | | Update Producteev | |
|---|---|---|---|---|---|---|---|---|---|

| Date | Details | | Billing | Person |
|---|---|---|---|---|
| ___/___/___ | Client: | | | |
| | | | Tel No | |
| | | | | |

| No Action | | Emailed | | Call Forward | | Client Task | | Update Producteev | |
|---|---|---|---|---|---|---|---|---|---|

| Date | Details | | Billing | Person |
|---|---|---|---|---|
| ___/___/___ | Client: | | | |
| | | | Tel No | |
| | | | | |
| No Action | | Emailed | | Call Forward | | Client Task | | Update Producteev | |

| Date | Details | | Billing | Person |
|---|---|---|---|---|
| ___/___/___ | Client: | | | |
| | | | Tel No | |
| | | | | |
| No Action | | Emailed | | Call Forward | | Client Task | | Update Producteev | |

| Date | Details | | Billing | Person |
|---|---|---|---|---|
| ___/___/___ | Client: | | | |
| | | | Tel No | |
| | | | | |
| No Action | | Emailed | | Call Forward | | Client Task | | Update Producteev | |

| Date | Details | | Billing | Person |
|---|---|---|---|---|
| ___/___/___ | Client: | | | |
| | | | Tel No | |
| | | | | |
| No Action | | Emailed | | Call Forward | | Client Task | | Update Producteev | |

| Date | Details | | Billing | Person |
|---|---|---|---|---|
| __/__/__ | Client: | | | |
| | | | Tel No | |
| | | | | |
| No Action | | Emailed | | Call Forward | | Client Task | | Update Producteev | |

| Date | Details | | Billing | Person |
|---|---|---|---|---|
| __/__/__ | Client: | | | |
| | | | Tel No | |
| | | | | |
| No Action | | Emailed | | Call Forward | | Client Task | | Update Producteev | |

| Date | Details | | Billing | Person |
|---|---|---|---|---|
| __/__/__ | Client: | | | |
| | | | Tel No | |
| | | | | |
| No Action | | Emailed | | Call Forward | | Client Task | | Update Producteev | |

| Date | Details | | Billing | Person |
|---|---|---|---|---|
| __/__/__ | Client: | | | |
| | | | Tel No | |
| | | | | |
| No Action | | Emailed | | Call Forward | | Client Task | | Update Producteev | |

| Date | Details | | Billing | Person |
|---|---|---|---|---|
| ___/___/___ | Client: | | | |
| | | | Tel No | |
| No Action | | Emailed | | Call Forward | | Client Task | | Update Producteev | |

| Date | Details | | Billing | Person |
|---|---|---|---|---|
| ___/___/___ | Client: | | | |
| | | | Tel No | |
| No Action | | Emailed | | Call Forward | | Client Task | | Update Producteev | |

| Date | Details | | Billing | Person |
|---|---|---|---|---|
| ___/___/___ | Client: | | | |
| | | | Tel No | |
| No Action | | Emailed | | Call Forward | | Client Task | | Update Producteev | |

| Date | Details | | Billing | Person |
|---|---|---|---|---|
| ___/___/___ | Client: | | | |
| | | | Tel No | |
| No Action | | Emailed | | Call Forward | | Client Task | | Update Producteev | |

| Date | Details | | Billing | Person |
|------|---------|---|---------|--------|
| __/__/__ | Client: | | | |
| | | | Tel No | |
| | _____ | | | |
| | _____ | | | |
| No Action | | Emailed | | Call Forward | | Client Task | | Update Producteev | |

| Date | Details | | Billing | Person |
|------|---------|---|---------|--------|
| __/__/__ | Client: | | | |
| | | | Tel No | |
| | _____ | | | |
| | _____ | | | |
| No Action | | Emailed | | Call Forward | | Client Task | | Update Producteev | |

| Date | Details | | Billing | Person |
|------|---------|---|---------|--------|
| __/__/__ | Client: | | | |
| | | | Tel No | |
| | _____ | | | |
| | _____ | | | |
| No Action | | Emailed | | Call Forward | | Client Task | | Update Producteev | |

| Date | Details | | Billing | Person |
|------|---------|---|---------|--------|
| __/__/__ | Client: | | | |
| | | | Tel No | |
| | _____ | | | |
| | _____ | | | |
| No Action | | Emailed | | Call Forward | | Client Task | | Update Producteev | |

| Date | Details | | Billing | Person |
|------|---------|---|---------|--------|
| ___/___/___ | Client: | | | |
| | | | Tel No | |
| | | | | |

| No Action | | Emailed | | Call Forward | | Client Task | | Update Producteev | |
|-----------|---|---------|---|--------------|---|-------------|---|-------------------|---|

| Date | Details | | Billing | Person |
|------|---------|---|---------|--------|
| ___/___/___ | Client: | | | |
| | | | Tel No | |
| | | | | |

| No Action | | Emailed | | Call Forward | | Client Task | | Update Producteev | |
|-----------|---|---------|---|--------------|---|-------------|---|-------------------|---|

| Date | Details | | Billing | Person |
|------|---------|---|---------|--------|
| ___/___/___ | Client: | | | |
| | | | Tel No | |
| | | | | |

| No Action | | Emailed | | Call Forward | | Client Task | | Update Producteev | |
|-----------|---|---------|---|--------------|---|-------------|---|-------------------|---|

| Date | Details | | Billing | Person |
|------|---------|---|---------|--------|
| ___/___/___ | Client: | | | |
| | | | Tel No | |
| | | | | |

| No Action | | Emailed | | Call Forward | | Client Task | | Update Producteev | |
|-----------|---|---------|---|--------------|---|-------------|---|-------------------|---|

| Date | Details | | Billing | Person |
|---|---|---|---|---|
| ___/___/___ | Client: | | | |
| | | | Tel No | |
| | _____ | | | |
| | _____ | | | |
| No Action | | Emailed | | Call Forward | | Client Task | | Update Producteev | |

| Date | Details | | Billing | Person |
|---|---|---|---|---|
| ___/___/___ | Client: | | | |
| | | | Tel No | |
| | _____ | | | |
| | _____ | | | |
| No Action | | Emailed | | Call Forward | | Client Task | | Update Producteev | |

| Date | Details | | Billing | Person |
|---|---|---|---|---|
| ___/___/___ | Client: | | | |
| | | | Tel No | |
| | _____ | | | |
| | _____ | | | |
| No Action | | Emailed | | Call Forward | | Client Task | | Update Producteev | |

| Date | Details | | Billing | Person |
|---|---|---|---|---|
| ___/___/___ | Client: | | | |
| | | | Tel No | |
| | _____ | | | |
| | _____ | | | |
| No Action | | Emailed | | Call Forward | | Client Task | | Update Producteev | |

| Date | Details | | Billing | Person |
|---|---|---|---|---|
| ___/___/___ | Client: | | | |
| | | | Tel No | |
| | | | | |

| No Action | | Emailed | | Call Forward | | Client Task | | Update Producteev | |
|---|---|---|---|---|---|---|---|---|---|

| Date | Details | | Billing | Person |
|---|---|---|---|---|
| ___/___/___ | Client: | | | |
| | | | Tel No | |
| | | | | |

| No Action | | Emailed | | Call Forward | | Client Task | | Update Producteev | |
|---|---|---|---|---|---|---|---|---|---|

| Date | Details | | Billing | Person |
|---|---|---|---|---|
| ___/___/___ | Client: | | | |
| | | | Tel No | |
| | | | | |

| No Action | | Emailed | | Call Forward | | Client Task | | Update Producteev | |
|---|---|---|---|---|---|---|---|---|---|

| Date | Details | | Billing | Person |
|---|---|---|---|---|
| ___/___/___ | Client: | | | |
| | | | Tel No | |
| | | | | |

| No Action | | Emailed | | Call Forward | | Client Task | | Update Producteev | |
|---|---|---|---|---|---|---|---|---|---|

| Date | Details | | Billing | Person |
|---|---|---|---|---|
| __/__/__ | Client: | | | |
| | | | Tel No | |
| | | | | |

| No Action | | Emailed | | Call Forward | | Client Task | | Update Producteev | |
|---|---|---|---|---|---|---|---|---|---|

| Date | Details | | Billing | Person |
|---|---|---|---|---|
| __/__/__ | Client: | | | |
| | | | Tel No | |
| | | | | |

| No Action | | Emailed | | Call Forward | | Client Task | | Update Producteev | |
|---|---|---|---|---|---|---|---|---|---|

| Date | Details | | Billing | Person |
|---|---|---|---|---|
| __/__/__ | Client: | | | |
| | | | Tel No | |
| | | | | |

| No Action | | Emailed | | Call Forward | | Client Task | | Update Producteev | |
|---|---|---|---|---|---|---|---|---|---|

| Date | Details | | Billing | Person |
|---|---|---|---|---|
| __/__/__ | Client: | | | |
| | | | Tel No | |
| | | | | |

| No Action | | Emailed | | Call Forward | | Client Task | | Update Producteev | |
|---|---|---|---|---|---|---|---|---|---|

| Date | Details | | Billing | Person |
|---|---|---|---|---|
| __/__/__ | Client: | | | |
| | | | Tel No | |
| | _____ | | | |
| | _____ | | | |
| No Action | | Emailed | Call Forward | Client Task | Update Producteev | |

| Date | Details | | Billing | Person |
|---|---|---|---|---|
| __/__/__ | Client: | | | |
| | | | Tel No | |
| | _____ | | | |
| | _____ | | | |
| No Action | | Emailed | Call Forward | Client Task | Update Producteev | |

| Date | Details | | Billing | Person |
|---|---|---|---|---|
| __/__/__ | Client: | | | |
| | | | Tel No | |
| | _____ | | | |
| | _____ | | | |
| No Action | | Emailed | Call Forward | Client Task | Update Producteev | |

| Date | Details | | Billing | Person |
|---|---|---|---|---|
| __/__/__ | Client: | | | |
| | | | Tel No | |
| | _____ | | | |
| | _____ | | | |
| No Action | | Emailed | Call Forward | Client Task | Update Producteev | |

| Date | Details | | Billing | Person |
|---|---|---|---|---|
| ___/___/___ | Client: | | | |
| | | Tel No | | |
| | | | | |
| No Action | | Emailed | | Call Forward | | Client Task | | Update Producteev | |

| Date | Details | | Billing | Person |
|---|---|---|---|---|
| ___/___/___ | Client: | | | |
| | | Tel No | | |
| | | | | |
| No Action | | Emailed | | Call Forward | | Client Task | | Update Producteev | |

| Date | Details | | Billing | Person |
|---|---|---|---|---|
| ___/___/___ | Client: | | | |
| | | Tel No | | |
| | | | | |
| No Action | | Emailed | | Call Forward | | Client Task | | Update Producteev | |

| Date | Details | | Billing | Person |
|---|---|---|---|---|
| ___/___/___ | Client: | | | |
| | | Tel No | | |
| | | | | |
| No Action | | Emailed | | Call Forward | | Client Task | | Update Producteev | |

| Date | Details | | Billing | Person |
|------|---------|---|---------|--------|
| __/__/__ | Client: | | | |
| | | | Tel No | |
| | | | | |
| No Action | | Emailed | | Call Forward | | Client Task | | Update Producteev | |

| Date | Details | | Billing | Person |
|------|---------|---|---------|--------|
| __/__/__ | Client: | | | |
| | | | Tel No | |
| | | | | |
| No Action | | Emailed | | Call Forward | | Client Task | | Update Producteev | |

| Date | Details | | Billing | Person |
|------|---------|---|---------|--------|
| __/__/__ | Client: | | | |
| | | | Tel No | |
| | | | | |
| No Action | | Emailed | | Call Forward | | Client Task | | Update Producteev | |

| Date | Details | | Billing | Person |
|------|---------|---|---------|--------|
| __/__/__ | Client: | | | |
| | | | Tel No | |
| | | | | |
| No Action | | Emailed | | Call Forward | | Client Task | | Update Producteev | |

| Date | Details | | Billing | Person |
|---|---|---|---|---|
| ___/___/___ | Client: | | | |
| | | | Tel No | |
| | _____ | | | |
| | _____ | | | |

| No Action | | Emailed | | Call Forward | | Client Task | | Update Producteev | |
|---|---|---|---|---|---|---|---|---|---|

| Date | Details | | Billing | Person |
|---|---|---|---|---|
| ___/___/___ | Client: | | | |
| | | | Tel No | |
| | _____ | | | |
| | _____ | | | |

| No Action | | Emailed | | Call Forward | | Client Task | | Update Producteev | |
|---|---|---|---|---|---|---|---|---|---|

| Date | Details | | Billing | Person |
|---|---|---|---|---|
| ___/___/___ | Client: | | | |
| | | | Tel No | |
| | _____ | | | |
| | _____ | | | |

| No Action | | Emailed | | Call Forward | | Client Task | | Update Producteev | |
|---|---|---|---|---|---|---|---|---|---|

| Date | Details | | Billing | Person |
|---|---|---|---|---|
| ___/___/___ | Client: | | | |
| | | | Tel No | |
| | _____ | | | |
| | _____ | | | |

| No Action | | Emailed | | Call Forward | | Client Task | | Update Producteev | |
|---|---|---|---|---|---|---|---|---|---|

| Date | Details | | Billing | Person |
|---|---|---|---|---|
| ___/___/___ | Client: | | | |
| | | | Tel No | |
| No Action | | Emailed | | Call Forward | | Client Task | | Update Producteev | |

| Date | Details | | Billing | Person |
|---|---|---|---|---|
| ___/___/___ | Client: | | | |
| | | | Tel No | |
| No Action | | Emailed | | Call Forward | | Client Task | | Update Producteev | |

| Date | Details | | Billing | Person |
|---|---|---|---|---|
| ___/___/___ | Client: | | | |
| | | | Tel No | |
| No Action | | Emailed | | Call Forward | | Client Task | | Update Producteev | |

| Date | Details | | Billing | Person |
|---|---|---|---|---|
| ___/___/___ | Client: | | | |
| | | | Tel No | |
| No Action | | Emailed | | Call Forward | | Client Task | | Update Producteev | |

| Date | Details | | Billing | Person |
|---|---|---|---|---|
| __/__/__ | Client: | | | |
| | | | Tel No | |
| | _____ | | | |
| | _____ | | | |

| No Action | | Emailed | | Call Forward | | Client Task | | Update Producteev | |
|---|---|---|---|---|---|---|---|---|---|

| Date | Details | | Billing | Person |
|---|---|---|---|---|
| __/__/__ | Client: | | | |
| | | | Tel No | |
| | _____ | | | |
| | _____ | | | |

| No Action | | Emailed | | Call Forward | | Client Task | | Update Producteev | |
|---|---|---|---|---|---|---|---|---|---|

| Date | Details | | Billing | Person |
|---|---|---|---|---|
| __/__/__ | Client: | | | |
| | | | Tel No | |
| | _____ | | | |
| | _____ | | | |

| No Action | | Emailed | | Call Forward | | Client Task | | Update Producteev | |
|---|---|---|---|---|---|---|---|---|---|

| Date | Details | | Billing | Person |
|---|---|---|---|---|
| __/__/__ | Client: | | | |
| | | | Tel No | |
| | _____ | | | |
| | _____ | | | |

| No Action | | Emailed | | Call Forward | | Client Task | | Update Producteev | |
|---|---|---|---|---|---|---|---|---|---|

| Date | Details | | Billing | Person |
|---|---|---|---|---|
| ___/___/___ | Client: | | | |
| | | | Tel No | |
| | | | | |
| No Action | | Emailed | | Call Forward | | Client Task | | Update Producteev | |

| Date | Details | | Billing | Person |
|---|---|---|---|---|
| ___/___/___ | Client: | | | |
| | | | Tel No | |
| | | | | |
| No Action | | Emailed | | Call Forward | | Client Task | | Update Producteev | |

| Date | Details | | Billing | Person |
|---|---|---|---|---|
| ___/___/___ | Client: | | | |
| | | | Tel No | |
| | | | | |
| No Action | | Emailed | | Call Forward | | Client Task | | Update Producteev | |

| Date | Details | | Billing | Person |
|---|---|---|---|---|
| ___/___/___ | Client: | | | |
| | | | Tel No | |
| | | | | |
| No Action | | Emailed | | Call Forward | | Client Task | | Update Producteev | |

| Date | Details | | Billing | Person |
|---|---|---|---|---|
| ___/___/___ | Client: | | | |
| | | | Tel No | |
| | | | | |
| No Action | | Emailed | | Call Forward | | Client Task | | Update Producteev | |

| Date | Details | | Billing | Person |
|---|---|---|---|---|
| ___/___/___ | Client: | | | |
| | | | Tel No | |
| | | | | |
| No Action | | Emailed | | Call Forward | | Client Task | | Update Producteev | |

| Date | Details | | Billing | Person |
|---|---|---|---|---|
| ___/___/___ | Client: | | | |
| | | | Tel No | |
| | | | | |
| No Action | | Emailed | | Call Forward | | Client Task | | Update Producteev | |

| Date | Details | | Billing | Person |
|---|---|---|---|---|
| ___/___/___ | Client: | | | |
| | | | Tel No | |
| | | | | |
| No Action | | Emailed | | Call Forward | | Client Task | | Update Producteev | |

| Date | Details | | Billing | Person |
|------|---------|---|---------|--------|
| __/__/__ | Client: | | | |
| | | | Tel No | |
| | | | | |
| No Action | | Emailed | | Call Forward | | Client Task | | Update Producteev | |

| Date | Details | | Billing | Person |
|------|---------|---|---------|--------|
| __/__/__ | Client: | | | |
| | | | Tel No | |
| | | | | |
| No Action | | Emailed | | Call Forward | | Client Task | | Update Producteev | |

| Date | Details | | Billing | Person |
|------|---------|---|---------|--------|
| __/__/__ | Client: | | | |
| | | | Tel No | |
| | | | | |
| No Action | | Emailed | | Call Forward | | Client Task | | Update Producteev | |

| Date | Details | | Billing | Person |
|------|---------|---|---------|--------|
| __/__/__ | Client: | | | |
| | | | Tel No | |
| | | | | |
| No Action | | Emailed | | Call Forward | | Client Task | | Update Producteev | |

| Date | Details | | Billing | Person |
|---|---|---|---|---|
| ___/___/___ | Client: | | | |
| | | | Tel No | |
| | _____ | | | |
| | _____ | | | |

| No Action | | Emailed | | Call Forward | | Client Task | | Update Producteev | |
|---|---|---|---|---|---|---|---|---|---|

| Date | Details | | Billing | Person |
|---|---|---|---|---|
| ___/___/___ | Client: | | | |
| | | | Tel No | |
| | _____ | | | |
| | _____ | | | |

| No Action | | Emailed | | Call Forward | | Client Task | | Update Producteev | |
|---|---|---|---|---|---|---|---|---|---|

| Date | Details | | Billing | Person |
|---|---|---|---|---|
| ___/___/___ | Client: | | | |
| | | | Tel No | |
| | _____ | | | |
| | _____ | | | |

| No Action | | Emailed | | Call Forward | | Client Task | | Update Producteev | |
|---|---|---|---|---|---|---|---|---|---|

| Date | Details | | Billing | Person |
|---|---|---|---|---|
| ___/___/___ | Client: | | | |
| | | | Tel No | |
| | _____ | | | |
| | _____ | | | |

| No Action | | Emailed | | Call Forward | | Client Task | | Update Producteev | |
|---|---|---|---|---|---|---|---|---|---|

| Date | Details | | Billing | Person |
|---|---|---|---|---|
| __/__/__ | Client: | | | |
| | | | Tel No | |
| | | | | |
| No Action | | Emailed | | Call Forward | | Client Task | | Update Producteev | |

| Date | Details | | Billing | Person |
|---|---|---|---|---|
| __/__/__ | Client: | | | |
| | | | Tel No | |
| | | | | |
| No Action | | Emailed | | Call Forward | | Client Task | | Update Producteev | |

| Date | Details | | Billing | Person |
|---|---|---|---|---|
| __/__/__ | Client: | | | |
| | | | Tel No | |
| | | | | |
| No Action | | Emailed | | Call Forward | | Client Task | | Update Producteev | |

| Date | Details | | Billing | Person |
|---|---|---|---|---|
| __/__/__ | Client: | | | |
| | | | Tel No | |
| | | | | |
| No Action | | Emailed | | Call Forward | | Client Task | | Update Producteev | |

| Date | Details | | Billing | Person |
|------|---------|---|---------|--------|
| ___/___/___ | Client: | | | |
| | | | Tel No | |
| | _____ | | | |
| | _____ | | | |

| No Action | | Emailed | | Call Forward | | Client Task | | Update Producteev | |
|-----------|--|---------|--|--------------|--|-------------|--|-------------------|--|

| Date | Details | | Billing | Person |
|------|---------|---|---------|--------|
| ___/___/___ | Client: | | | |
| | | | Tel No | |
| | _____ | | | |
| | _____ | | | |

| No Action | | Emailed | | Call Forward | | Client Task | | Update Producteev | |
|-----------|--|---------|--|--------------|--|-------------|--|-------------------|--|

| Date | Details | | Billing | Person |
|------|---------|---|---------|--------|
| ___/___/___ | Client: | | | |
| | | | Tel No | |
| | _____ | | | |
| | _____ | | | |

| No Action | | Emailed | | Call Forward | | Client Task | | Update Producteev | |
|-----------|--|---------|--|--------------|--|-------------|--|-------------------|--|

| Date | Details | | Billing | Person |
|------|---------|---|---------|--------|
| ___/___/___ | Client: | | | |
| | | | Tel No | |
| | _____ | | | |
| | _____ | | | |

| No Action | | Emailed | | Call Forward | | Client Task | | Update Producteev | |
|-----------|--|---------|--|--------------|--|-------------|--|-------------------|--|

| Date | Details | | Billing | Person |
|------|---------|---|---------|--------|
| ___/___/___ | Client: | | | |
| | | | Tel No | |
| | _____ | | | |
| | _____ | | | |
| No Action | | Emailed | | Call Forward | | Client Task | | Update Producteev | |

| Date | Details | | Billing | Person |
|------|---------|---|---------|--------|
| ___/___/___ | Client: | | | |
| | | | Tel No | |
| | _____ | | | |
| | _____ | | | |
| No Action | | Emailed | | Call Forward | | Client Task | | Update Producteev | |

| Date | Details | | Billing | Person |
|------|---------|---|---------|--------|
| ___/___/___ | Client: | | | |
| | | | Tel No | |
| | _____ | | | |
| | _____ | | | |
| No Action | | Emailed | | Call Forward | | Client Task | | Update Producteev | |

| Date | Details | | Billing | Person |
|------|---------|---|---------|--------|
| ___/___/___ | Client: | | | |
| | | | Tel No | |
| | _____ | | | |
| | _____ | | | |
| No Action | | Emailed | | Call Forward | | Client Task | | Update Producteev | |

| Date | Details | | Billing | Person |
|---|---|---|---|---|
| ___/___/___ | Client: | | | |
| | | Tel No | | |
| | | | | |
| No Action | | Emailed | | Call Forward | | Client Task | | Update Producteev | |

| Date | Details | | Billing | Person |
|---|---|---|---|---|
| ___/___/___ | Client: | | | |
| | | Tel No | | |
| | | | | |
| No Action | | Emailed | | Call Forward | | Client Task | | Update Producteev | |

| Date | Details | | Billing | Person |
|---|---|---|---|---|
| ___/___/___ | Client: | | | |
| | | Tel No | | |
| | | | | |
| No Action | | Emailed | | Call Forward | | Client Task | | Update Producteev | |

| Date | Details | | Billing | Person |
|---|---|---|---|---|
| ___/___/___ | Client: | | | |
| | | Tel No | | |
| | | | | |
| No Action | | Emailed | | Call Forward | | Client Task | | Update Producteev | |

| Date | Details | | Billing | Person |
|---|---|---|---|---|
| __/__/__ | Client: | | | |
| | | | Tel No | |
| | | | | |
| No Action | | Emailed | | Call Forward | | Client Task | | Update Producteev | |

| Date | Details | | Billing | Person |
|---|---|---|---|---|
| __/__/__ | Client: | | | |
| | | | Tel No | |
| | | | | |
| No Action | | Emailed | | Call Forward | | Client Task | | Update Producteev | |

| Date | Details | | Billing | Person |
|---|---|---|---|---|
| __/__/__ | Client: | | | |
| | | | Tel No | |
| | | | | |
| No Action | | Emailed | | Call Forward | | Client Task | | Update Producteev | |

| Date | Details | | Billing | Person |
|---|---|---|---|---|
| __/__/__ | Client: | | | |
| | | | Tel No | |
| | | | | |
| No Action | | Emailed | | Call Forward | | Client Task | | Update Producteev | |

| Date | Details | | Billing | Person |
|---|---|---|---|---|
| ___/___/___ | Client: | | | |
| | | | Tel No | |
| | | | | |
| No Action | | Emailed | | Call Forward | | Client Task | | Update Producteev | |

| Date | Details | | Billing | Person |
|---|---|---|---|---|
| ___/___/___ | Client: | | | |
| | | | Tel No | |
| | | | | |
| No Action | | Emailed | | Call Forward | | Client Task | | Update Producteev | |

| Date | Details | | Billing | Person |
|---|---|---|---|---|
| ___/___/___ | Client: | | | |
| | | | Tel No | |
| | | | | |
| No Action | | Emailed | | Call Forward | | Client Task | | Update Producteev | |

| Date | Details | | Billing | Person |
|---|---|---|---|---|
| ___/___/___ | Client: | | | |
| | | | Tel No | |
| | | | | |
| No Action | | Emailed | | Call Forward | | Client Task | | Update Producteev | |

| Date | Details | | Billing | Person |
|---|---|---|---|---|
| __/__/__ | Client: | | | |
| | | | Tel No | |
| No Action | | Emailed | | Call Forward | | Client Task | | Update Producteev | |

| Date | Details | | Billing | Person |
|---|---|---|---|---|
| __/__/__ | Client: | | | |
| | | | Tel No | |
| No Action | | Emailed | | Call Forward | | Client Task | | Update Producteev | |

| Date | Details | | Billing | Person |
|---|---|---|---|---|
| __/__/__ | Client: | | | |
| | | | Tel No | |
| No Action | | Emailed | | Call Forward | | Client Task | | Update Producteev | |

| Date | Details | | Billing | Person |
|---|---|---|---|---|
| __/__/__ | Client: | | | |
| | | | Tel No | |
| No Action | | Emailed | | Call Forward | | Client Task | | Update Producteev | |

| Date | Details | | | | | | Billing | Person |
|---|---|---|---|---|---|---|---|---|
| ___/___/___ | Client: | | | | | | | |
| | | | | | | | Tel No | |
| | _____ | | | | | | | |
| | _____ | | | | | | | |
| No Action | | Emailed | | Call Forward | | Client Task | | Update Producteev | |

| Date | Details | | | | | | Billing | Person |
|---|---|---|---|---|---|---|---|---|
| ___/___/___ | Client: | | | | | | | |
| | | | | | | | Tel No | |
| | _____ | | | | | | | |
| | _____ | | | | | | | |
| No Action | | Emailed | | Call Forward | | Client Task | | Update Producteev | |

| Date | Details | | | | | | Billing | Person |
|---|---|---|---|---|---|---|---|---|
| ___/___/___ | Client: | | | | | | | |
| | | | | | | | Tel No | |
| | _____ | | | | | | | |
| | _____ | | | | | | | |
| No Action | | Emailed | | Call Forward | | Client Task | | Update Producteev | |

| Date | Details | | | | | | Billing | Person |
|---|---|---|---|---|---|---|---|---|
| ___/___/___ | Client: | | | | | | | |
| | | | | | | | Tel No | |
| | _____ | | | | | | | |
| | _____ | | | | | | | |
| No Action | | Emailed | | Call Forward | | Client Task | | Update Producteev | |

| Date | Details | | Billing | Person |
|------|---------|---|---------|--------|
| __/__/__ | Client: | | | |
| | | | Tel No | |
| | | | | |
| No Action | | Emailed | | Call Forward | | Client Task | | Update Producteev | |

| Date | Details | | Billing | Person |
|------|---------|---|---------|--------|
| __/__/__ | Client: | | | |
| | | | Tel No | |
| | | | | |
| No Action | | Emailed | | Call Forward | | Client Task | | Update Producteev | |

| Date | Details | | Billing | Person |
|------|---------|---|---------|--------|
| __/__/__ | Client: | | | |
| | | | Tel No | |
| | | | | |
| No Action | | Emailed | | Call Forward | | Client Task | | Update Producteev | |

| Date | Details | | Billing | Person |
|------|---------|---|---------|--------|
| __/__/__ | Client: | | | |
| | | | Tel No | |
| | | | | |
| No Action | | Emailed | | Call Forward | | Client Task | | Update Producteev | |

| Date | Details | | Billing | Person |
|---|---|---|---|---|
| ___/___/___ | Client: | | | |
| | | | Tel No | |
| | _____ | | | |
| | _____ | | | |
| No Action | | Emailed | | Call Forward | | Client Task | | Update Producteev | |

| Date | Details | | Billing | Person |
|---|---|---|---|---|
| ___/___/___ | Client: | | | |
| | | | Tel No | |
| | _____ | | | |
| | _____ | | | |
| No Action | | Emailed | | Call Forward | | Client Task | | Update Producteev | |

| Date | Details | | Billing | Person |
|---|---|---|---|---|
| ___/___/___ | Client: | | | |
| | | | Tel No | |
| | _____ | | | |
| | _____ | | | |
| No Action | | Emailed | | Call Forward | | Client Task | | Update Producteev | |

| Date | Details | | Billing | Person |
|---|---|---|---|---|
| ___/___/___ | Client: | | | |
| | | | Tel No | |
| | _____ | | | |
| | _____ | | | |
| No Action | | Emailed | | Call Forward | | Client Task | | Update Producteev | |

| Date | Details | | Billing | Person |
|---|---|---|---|---|
| ___/___/___ | Client: | | | |
| | | | Tel No | |
| | | | | |
| No Action | | Emailed | | Call Forward | | Client Task | | Update Producteev | |

| Date | Details | | Billing | Person |
|---|---|---|---|---|
| ___/___/___ | Client: | | | |
| | | | Tel No | |
| | | | | |
| No Action | | Emailed | | Call Forward | | Client Task | | Update Producteev | |

| Date | Details | | Billing | Person |
|---|---|---|---|---|
| ___/___/___ | Client: | | | |
| | | | Tel No | |
| | | | | |
| No Action | | Emailed | | Call Forward | | Client Task | | Update Producteev | |

| Date | Details | | Billing | Person |
|---|---|---|---|---|
| ___/___/___ | Client: | | | |
| | | | Tel No | |
| | | | | |
| No Action | | Emailed | | Call Forward | | Client Task | | Update Producteev | |

| Date | Details | | Billing | Person |
|------|---------|---|---------|--------|
| ___/___/___ | Client: | | | |
| | | | Tel No | |
| | _____ | | | |
| | _____ | | | |
| No Action | | Emailed | | Call Forward | | Client Task | | Update Producteev | |

| Date | Details | | Billing | Person |
|------|---------|---|---------|--------|
| ___/___/___ | Client: | | | |
| | | | Tel No | |
| | _____ | | | |
| | _____ | | | |
| No Action | | Emailed | | Call Forward | | Client Task | | Update Producteev | |

| Date | Details | | Billing | Person |
|------|---------|---|---------|--------|
| ___/___/___ | Client: | | | |
| | | | Tel No | |
| | _____ | | | |
| | _____ | | | |
| No Action | | Emailed | | Call Forward | | Client Task | | Update Producteev | |

| Date | Details | | Billing | Person |
|------|---------|---|---------|--------|
| ___/___/___ | Client: | | | |
| | | | Tel No | |
| | _____ | | | |
| | _____ | | | |
| No Action | | Emailed | | Call Forward | | Client Task | | Update Producteev | |

| Date | Details | | Billing | Person |
|---|---|---|---|---|
| ___/___/___ | Client: | | | |
| | | | Tel No | |
| | | | | |
| No Action | | Emailed | | Call Forward | | Client Task | | Update Producteev | |

| Date | Details | | Billing | Person |
|---|---|---|---|---|
| ___/___/___ | Client: | | | |
| | | | Tel No | |
| | | | | |
| No Action | | Emailed | | Call Forward | | Client Task | | Update Producteev | |

| Date | Details | | Billing | Person |
|---|---|---|---|---|
| ___/___/___ | Client: | | | |
| | | | Tel No | |
| | | | | |
| No Action | | Emailed | | Call Forward | | Client Task | | Update Producteev | |

| Date | Details | | Billing | Person |
|---|---|---|---|---|
| ___/___/___ | Client: | | | |
| | | | Tel No | |
| | | | | |
| No Action | | Emailed | | Call Forward | | Client Task | | Update Producteev | |

| Date | Details | | Billing | Person |
|---|---|---|---|---|
| ___/___/___ | Client: | | | |
| | | | Tel No | |
| No Action | | Emailed | | Call Forward | | Client Task | | Update Producteev | |

| Date | Details | | Billing | Person |
|---|---|---|---|---|
| ___/___/___ | Client: | | | |
| | | | Tel No | |
| No Action | | Emailed | | Call Forward | | Client Task | | Update Producteev | |

| Date | Details | | Billing | Person |
|---|---|---|---|---|
| ___/___/___ | Client: | | | |
| | | | Tel No | |
| No Action | | Emailed | | Call Forward | | Client Task | | Update Producteev | |

| Date | Details | | Billing | Person |
|---|---|---|---|---|
| ___/___/___ | Client: | | | |
| | | | Tel No | |
| No Action | | Emailed | | Call Forward | | Client Task | | Update Producteev | |

| Date | Details | | Billing | Person |
|------|---------|---|---------|--------|
| ___/___/___ | Client: | | | |
| | | | Tel No | |
| | _____ | | | |
| | _____ | | | |

| No Action | | Emailed | | Call Forward | | Client Task | | Update Producteev | |
|-----------|--|---------|--|--------------|--|-------------|--|-------------------|--|

| Date | Details | | Billing | Person |
|------|---------|---|---------|--------|
| ___/___/___ | Client: | | | |
| | | | Tel No | |
| | _____ | | | |
| | _____ | | | |

| No Action | | Emailed | | Call Forward | | Client Task | | Update Producteev | |
|-----------|--|---------|--|--------------|--|-------------|--|-------------------|--|

| Date | Details | | Billing | Person |
|------|---------|---|---------|--------|
| ___/___/___ | Client: | | | |
| | | | Tel No | |
| | _____ | | | |
| | _____ | | | |

| No Action | | Emailed | | Call Forward | | Client Task | | Update Producteev | |
|-----------|--|---------|--|--------------|--|-------------|--|-------------------|--|

| Date | Details | | Billing | Person |
|------|---------|---|---------|--------|
| ___/___/___ | Client: | | | |
| | | | Tel No | |
| | _____ | | | |
| | _____ | | | |

| No Action | | Emailed | | Call Forward | | Client Task | | Update Producteev | |
|-----------|--|---------|--|--------------|--|-------------|--|-------------------|--|

| Date | Details | | Billing | Person |
|---|---|---|---|---|
| ___/___/___ | Client: | | | |
| | | | Tel No | |
| | | | | |
| No Action | | Emailed | | Call Forward | | Client Task | | Update Producteev | |

| Date | Details | | Billing | Person |
|---|---|---|---|---|
| ___/___/___ | Client: | | | |
| | | | Tel No | |
| | | | | |
| No Action | | Emailed | | Call Forward | | Client Task | | Update Producteev | |

| Date | Details | | Billing | Person |
|---|---|---|---|---|
| ___/___/___ | Client: | | | |
| | | | Tel No | |
| | | | | |
| No Action | | Emailed | | Call Forward | | Client Task | | Update Producteev | |

| Date | Details | | Billing | Person |
|---|---|---|---|---|
| ___/___/___ | Client: | | | |
| | | | Tel No | |
| | | | | |
| No Action | | Emailed | | Call Forward | | Client Task | | Update Producteev | |

| Date | Details | | Billing | Person |
|---|---|---|---|---|
| __/__/__ | Client: | | | |
| | | | Tel No | |
| | | | | |
| No Action | | Emailed | | Call Forward | | Client Task | | Update Producteev | |

| Date | Details | | Billing | Person |
|---|---|---|---|---|
| __/__/__ | Client: | | | |
| | | | Tel No | |
| | | | | |
| No Action | | Emailed | | Call Forward | | Client Task | | Update Producteev | |

| Date | Details | | Billing | Person |
|---|---|---|---|---|
| __/__/__ | Client: | | | |
| | | | Tel No | |
| | | | | |
| No Action | | Emailed | | Call Forward | | Client Task | | Update Producteev | |

| Date | Details | | Billing | Person |
|---|---|---|---|---|
| __/__/__ | Client: | | | |
| | | | Tel No | |
| | | | | |
| No Action | | Emailed | | Call Forward | | Client Task | | Update Producteev | |

| Date | Details | | Billing | Person |
|---|---|---|---|---|
| ___/___/___ | Client: | | | |
| | | Tel No | | |
| | _____ | | | |
| | _____ | | | |
| No Action | | Emailed | | Call Forward | | Client Task | | Update Producteev | |

| Date | Details | | Billing | Person |
|---|---|---|---|---|
| ___/___/___ | Client: | | | |
| | | Tel No | | |
| | _____ | | | |
| | _____ | | | |
| No Action | | Emailed | | Call Forward | | Client Task | | Update Producteev | |

| Date | Details | | Billing | Person |
|---|---|---|---|---|
| ___/___/___ | Client: | | | |
| | | Tel No | | |
| | _____ | | | |
| | _____ | | | |
| No Action | | Emailed | | Call Forward | | Client Task | | Update Producteev | |

| Date | Details | | Billing | Person |
|---|---|---|---|---|
| ___/___/___ | Client: | | | |
| | | Tel No | | |
| | _____ | | | |
| | _____ | | | |
| No Action | | Emailed | | Call Forward | | Client Task | | Update Producteev | |

| Date | Details | | Billing | Person |
|---|---|---|---|---|
| ___/___/___ | Client: | | | |
| | | | Tel No | |
| | | | | |
| No Action | | Emailed | | Call Forward | | Client Task | | Update Producteev | |

| Date | Details | | Billing | Person |
|---|---|---|---|---|
| ___/___/___ | Client: | | | |
| | | | Tel No | |
| | | | | |
| No Action | | Emailed | | Call Forward | | Client Task | | Update Producteev | |

| Date | Details | | Billing | Person |
|---|---|---|---|---|
| ___/___/___ | Client: | | | |
| | | | Tel No | |
| | | | | |
| No Action | | Emailed | | Call Forward | | Client Task | | Update Producteev | |

| Date | Details | | Billing | Person |
|---|---|---|---|---|
| ___/___/___ | Client: | | | |
| | | | Tel No | |
| | | | | |
| No Action | | Emailed | | Call Forward | | Client Task | | Update Producteev | |

| Date | Details | | Billing | Person |
|---|---|---|---|---|
| ___/___/___ | Client: | | | |
| | | | Tel No | |
| | | | | |

| No Action | | Emailed | | Call Forward | | Client Task | | Update Producteev | |
|---|---|---|---|---|---|---|---|---|---|

| Date | Details | | Billing | Person |
|---|---|---|---|---|
| ___/___/___ | Client: | | | |
| | | | Tel No | |
| | | | | |

| No Action | | Emailed | | Call Forward | | Client Task | | Update Producteev | |
|---|---|---|---|---|---|---|---|---|---|

| Date | Details | | Billing | Person |
|---|---|---|---|---|
| ___/___/___ | Client: | | | |
| | | | Tel No | |
| | | | | |

| No Action | | Emailed | | Call Forward | | Client Task | | Update Producteev | |
|---|---|---|---|---|---|---|---|---|---|

| Date | Details | | Billing | Person |
|---|---|---|---|---|
| ___/___/___ | Client: | | | |
| | | | Tel No | |
| | | | | |

| No Action | | Emailed | | Call Forward | | Client Task | | Update Producteev | |
|---|---|---|---|---|---|---|---|---|---|

| Date | Details | | Billing | Person |
|------|---------|---|---------|--------|
| ___/___/___ | Client: | | | |
| | | | Tel No | |
| | | | | |
| No Action | | Emailed | | Call Forward | | Client Task | | Update Producteev | |

| Date | Details | | Billing | Person |
|------|---------|---|---------|--------|
| ___/___/___ | Client: | | | |
| | | | Tel No | |
| | | | | |
| No Action | | Emailed | | Call Forward | | Client Task | | Update Producteev | |

| Date | Details | | Billing | Person |
|------|---------|---|---------|--------|
| ___/___/___ | Client: | | | |
| | | | Tel No | |
| | | | | |
| No Action | | Emailed | | Call Forward | | Client Task | | Update Producteev | |

| Date | Details | | Billing | Person |
|------|---------|---|---------|--------|
| ___/___/___ | Client: | | | |
| | | | Tel No | |
| | | | | |
| No Action | | Emailed | | Call Forward | | Client Task | | Update Producteev | |

| Date | Details | | Billing | Person |
|------|---------|---|---------|--------|
| ___/___/___ | Client: | | | |
| | | | Tel No | |
| | | | | |

| No Action | | Emailed | | Call Forward | | Client Task | | Update Producteev | |
|-----------|--|---------|--|--------------|--|-------------|--|-------------------|--|

| Date | Details | | Billing | Person |
|------|---------|---|---------|--------|
| ___/___/___ | Client: | | | |
| | | | Tel No | |
| | | | | |

| No Action | | Emailed | | Call Forward | | Client Task | | Update Producteev | |
|-----------|--|---------|--|--------------|--|-------------|--|-------------------|--|

| Date | Details | | Billing | Person |
|------|---------|---|---------|--------|
| ___/___/___ | Client: | | | |
| | | | Tel No | |
| | | | | |

| No Action | | Emailed | | Call Forward | | Client Task | | Update Producteev | |
|-----------|--|---------|--|--------------|--|-------------|--|-------------------|--|

| Date | Details | | Billing | Person |
|------|---------|---|---------|--------|
| ___/___/___ | Client: | | | |
| | | | Tel No | |
| | | | | |

| No Action | | Emailed | | Call Forward | | Client Task | | Update Producteev | |
|-----------|--|---------|--|--------------|--|-------------|--|-------------------|--|

| Date | Details | | Billing | Person |
|---|---|---|---|---|
| __/__/__ | Client: | | | |
| | | | Tel No | |
| | | | | |
| No Action | | Emailed | | Call Forward | | Client Task | | Update Producteev | |

| Date | Details | | Billing | Person |
|---|---|---|---|---|
| __/__/__ | Client: | | | |
| | | | Tel No | |
| | | | | |
| No Action | | Emailed | | Call Forward | | Client Task | | Update Producteev | |

| Date | Details | | Billing | Person |
|---|---|---|---|---|
| __/__/__ | Client: | | | |
| | | | Tel No | |
| | | | | |
| No Action | | Emailed | | Call Forward | | Client Task | | Update Producteev | |

| Date | Details | | Billing | Person |
|---|---|---|---|---|
| __/__/__ | Client: | | | |
| | | | Tel No | |
| | | | | |
| No Action | | Emailed | | Call Forward | | Client Task | | Update Producteev | |

| Date | Details | | Billing | Person |
|------|---------|---|---------|--------|
| ___/___/___ | Client: | | | |
| | | | Tel No | |
| | _____ | | | |
| | _____ | | | |
| | | | | |

| No Action | | Emailed | | Call Forward | | Client Task | | Update Producteev | |
|-----------|---|---------|---|--------------|---|-------------|---|-------------------|---|

| Date | Details | | Billing | Person |
|------|---------|---|---------|--------|
| ___/___/___ | Client: | | | |
| | | | Tel No | |
| | _____ | | | |
| | _____ | | | |
| | | | | |

| No Action | | Emailed | | Call Forward | | Client Task | | Update Producteev | |
|-----------|---|---------|---|--------------|---|-------------|---|-------------------|---|

| Date | Details | | Billing | Person |
|------|---------|---|---------|--------|
| ___/___/___ | Client: | | | |
| | | | Tel No | |
| | _____ | | | |
| | _____ | | | |
| | | | | |

| No Action | | Emailed | | Call Forward | | Client Task | | Update Producteev | |
|-----------|---|---------|---|--------------|---|-------------|---|-------------------|---|

| Date | Details | | Billing | Person |
|------|---------|---|---------|--------|
| ___/___/___ | Client: | | | |
| | | | Tel No | |
| | _____ | | | |
| | _____ | | | |
| | | | | |

| No Action | | Emailed | | Call Forward | | Client Task | | Update Producteev | |
|-----------|---|---------|---|--------------|---|-------------|---|-------------------|---|

| Date | Details | | Billing | Person |
|---|---|---|---|---|
| __/__/__ | Client: | | | |
| | | | Tel No | |
| | | | | |
| No Action | | Emailed | | Call Forward | | Client Task | | Update Producteev | |

| Date | Details | | Billing | Person |
|---|---|---|---|---|
| __/__/__ | Client: | | | |
| | | | Tel No | |
| | | | | |
| No Action | | Emailed | | Call Forward | | Client Task | | Update Producteev | |

| Date | Details | | Billing | Person |
|---|---|---|---|---|
| __/__/__ | Client: | | | |
| | | | Tel No | |
| | | | | |
| No Action | | Emailed | | Call Forward | | Client Task | | Update Producteev | |

| Date | Details | | Billing | Person |
|---|---|---|---|---|
| __/__/__ | Client: | | | |
| | | | Tel No | |
| | | | | |
| No Action | | Emailed | | Call Forward | | Client Task | | Update Producteev | |

| Date | Details | | Billing | Person |
|---|---|---|---|---|
| ___/___/___ | Client: | | | |
| | | | Tel No | |
| | | | | |

| No Action | | Emailed | | Call Forward | | Client Task | | Update Producteev | |
|---|---|---|---|---|---|---|---|---|---|

| Date | Details | | Billing | Person |
|---|---|---|---|---|
| ___/___/___ | Client: | | | |
| | | | Tel No | |
| | | | | |

| No Action | | Emailed | | Call Forward | | Client Task | | Update Producteev | |
|---|---|---|---|---|---|---|---|---|---|

| Date | Details | | Billing | Person |
|---|---|---|---|---|
| ___/___/___ | Client: | | | |
| | | | Tel No | |
| | | | | |

| No Action | | Emailed | | Call Forward | | Client Task | | Update Producteev | |
|---|---|---|---|---|---|---|---|---|---|

| Date | Details | | Billing | Person |
|---|---|---|---|---|
| ___/___/___ | Client: | | | |
| | | | Tel No | |
| | | | | |

| No Action | | Emailed | | Call Forward | | Client Task | | Update Producteev | |
|---|---|---|---|---|---|---|---|---|---|

| Date | Details | | Billing | Person |
|---|---|---|---|---|
| __/__/__ | Client: | | | |
| | | | Tel No | |
| | | | | |
| No Action | | Emailed | Call Forward | Client Task | Update Producteev | |

| Date | Details | | Billing | Person |
|---|---|---|---|---|
| __/__/__ | Client: | | | |
| | | | Tel No | |
| | | | | |
| No Action | | Emailed | Call Forward | Client Task | Update Producteev | |

| Date | Details | | Billing | Person |
|---|---|---|---|---|
| __/__/__ | Client: | | | |
| | | | Tel No | |
| | | | | |
| No Action | | Emailed | Call Forward | Client Task | Update Producteev | |

| Date | Details | | Billing | Person |
|---|---|---|---|---|
| __/__/__ | Client: | | | |
| | | | Tel No | |
| | | | | |
| No Action | | Emailed | Call Forward | Client Task | Update Producteev | |

| Date | Details | | Billing | Person |
|------|---------|---|---------|--------|
| ___/___/___ | Client: | | | |
| | | | Tel No | |
| | | | | |
| | | | | |

| No Action | | Emailed | | Call Forward | | Client Task | | Update Producteev | |
|-----------|---|---------|---|--------------|---|-------------|---|-------------------|---|

| Date | Details | | Billing | Person |
|------|---------|---|---------|--------|
| ___/___/___ | Client: | | | |
| | | | Tel No | |
| | | | | |
| | | | | |

| No Action | | Emailed | | Call Forward | | Client Task | | Update Producteev | |
|-----------|---|---------|---|--------------|---|-------------|---|-------------------|---|

| Date | Details | | Billing | Person |
|------|---------|---|---------|--------|
| ___/___/___ | Client: | | | |
| | | | Tel No | |
| | | | | |
| | | | | |

| No Action | | Emailed | | Call Forward | | Client Task | | Update Producteev | |
|-----------|---|---------|---|--------------|---|-------------|---|-------------------|---|

| Date | Details | | Billing | Person |
|------|---------|---|---------|--------|
| ___/___/___ | Client: | | | |
| | | | Tel No | |
| | | | | |
| | | | | |

| No Action | | Emailed | | Call Forward | | Client Task | | Update Producteev | |
|-----------|---|---------|---|--------------|---|-------------|---|-------------------|---|

| Date | Details | | Billing | Person |
|---|---|---|---|---|
| ___/___/___ | Client: | | | |
| | | | Tel No | |
| No Action | | Emailed | | Call Forward | | Client Task | | Update Producteev | |

| Date | Details | | Billing | Person |
|---|---|---|---|---|
| ___/___/___ | Client: | | | |
| | | | Tel No | |
| No Action | | Emailed | | Call Forward | | Client Task | | Update Producteev | |

| Date | Details | | Billing | Person |
|---|---|---|---|---|
| ___/___/___ | Client: | | | |
| | | | Tel No | |
| No Action | | Emailed | | Call Forward | | Client Task | | Update Producteev | |

| Date | Details | | Billing | Person |
|---|---|---|---|---|
| ___/___/___ | Client: | | | |
| | | | Tel No | |
| No Action | | Emailed | | Call Forward | | Client Task | | Update Producteev | |

| Date | Details | | Billing | Person |
|---|---|---|---|---|
| ___/___/___ | Client: | | | |
| | | | Tel No | |
| No Action | | Emailed | Call Forward | Client Task | Update Producteev |

| Date | Details | | Billing | Person |
|---|---|---|---|---|
| ___/___/___ | Client: | | | |
| | | | Tel No | |
| No Action | | Emailed | Call Forward | Client Task | Update Producteev |

| Date | Details | | Billing | Person |
|---|---|---|---|---|
| ___/___/___ | Client: | | | |
| | | | Tel No | |
| No Action | | Emailed | Call Forward | Client Task | Update Producteev |

| Date | Details | | Billing | Person |
|---|---|---|---|---|
| ___/___/___ | Client: | | | |
| | | | Tel No | |
| No Action | | Emailed | Call Forward | Client Task | Update Producteev |

| Date | Details | | Billing | Person |
|---|---|---|---|---|
| __/__/__ | Client: | | | |
| | | | Tel No | |
| No Action | | Emailed | Call Forward | Client Task | Update Producteev | |

| Date | Details | | Billing | Person |
|---|---|---|---|---|
| __/__/__ | Client: | | | |
| | | | Tel No | |
| No Action | | Emailed | Call Forward | Client Task | Update Producteev | |

| Date | Details | | Billing | Person |
|---|---|---|---|---|
| __/__/__ | Client: | | | |
| | | | Tel No | |
| No Action | | Emailed | Call Forward | Client Task | Update Producteev | |

| Date | Details | | Billing | Person |
|---|---|---|---|---|
| __/__/__ | Client: | | | |
| | | | Tel No | |
| No Action | | Emailed | Call Forward | Client Task | Update Producteev | |

| Date | Details | | Billing | Person |
|---|---|---|---|---|
| ___/___/___ | Client: | | | |
| | | | Tel No | |
| | _____ | | | |
| | _____ | | | |
| No Action | | Emailed | | Call Forward | | Client Task | | Update Producteev | |

| Date | Details | | Billing | Person |
|---|---|---|---|---|
| ___/___/___ | Client: | | | |
| | | | Tel No | |
| | _____ | | | |
| | _____ | | | |
| No Action | | Emailed | | Call Forward | | Client Task | | Update Producteev | |

| Date | Details | | Billing | Person |
|---|---|---|---|---|
| ___/___/___ | Client: | | | |
| | | | Tel No | |
| | _____ | | | |
| | _____ | | | |
| No Action | | Emailed | | Call Forward | | Client Task | | Update Producteev | |

| Date | Details | | Billing | Person |
|---|---|---|---|---|
| ___/___/___ | Client: | | | |
| | | | Tel No | |
| | _____ | | | |
| | _____ | | | |
| No Action | | Emailed | | Call Forward | | Client Task | | Update Producteev | |

| Date | Details | | Billing | Person |
|---|---|---|---|---|
| __/__/__ | Client: | | | |
| | | | Tel No | |
| No Action | | Emailed | | Call Forward | | Client Task | | Update Producteev | |

| Date | Details | | Billing | Person |
|---|---|---|---|---|
| __/__/__ | Client: | | | |
| | | | Tel No | |
| No Action | | Emailed | | Call Forward | | Client Task | | Update Producteev | |

| Date | Details | | Billing | Person |
|---|---|---|---|---|
| __/__/__ | Client: | | | |
| | | | Tel No | |
| No Action | | Emailed | | Call Forward | | Client Task | | Update Producteev | |

| Date | Details | | Billing | Person |
|---|---|---|---|---|
| __/__/__ | Client: | | | |
| | | | Tel No | |
| No Action | | Emailed | | Call Forward | | Client Task | | Update Producteev | |

| Date | Details | | Billing | Person |
|---|---|---|---|---|
| ___/___/___ | Client: | | | |
| | | Tel No | | |
| | _____ | | | |
| | _____ | | | |

| No Action | | Emailed | | Call Forward | | Client Task | | Update Producteev | |
|---|---|---|---|---|---|---|---|---|---|

| Date | Details | | Billing | Person |
|---|---|---|---|---|
| ___/___/___ | Client: | | | |
| | | Tel No | | |
| | _____ | | | |
| | _____ | | | |

| No Action | | Emailed | | Call Forward | | Client Task | | Update Producteev | |
|---|---|---|---|---|---|---|---|---|---|

| Date | Details | | Billing | Person |
|---|---|---|---|---|
| ___/___/___ | Client: | | | |
| | | Tel No | | |
| | _____ | | | |
| | _____ | | | |

| No Action | | Emailed | | Call Forward | | Client Task | | Update Producteev | |
|---|---|---|---|---|---|---|---|---|---|

| Date | Details | | Billing | Person |
|---|---|---|---|---|
| ___/___/___ | Client: | | | |
| | | Tel No | | |
| | _____ | | | |
| | _____ | | | |

| No Action | | Emailed | | Call Forward | | Client Task | | Update Producteev | |
|---|---|---|---|---|---|---|---|---|---|

| Date | Details | | Billing | Person |
|---|---|---|---|---|
| ___/___/___ | Client: | | | |
| | | | Tel No | |
| | | | | |
| No Action | | Emailed | | Call Forward | | Client Task | | Update Producteev | |

| Date | Details | | Billing | Person |
|---|---|---|---|---|
| ___/___/___ | Client: | | | |
| | | | Tel No | |
| | | | | |
| No Action | | Emailed | | Call Forward | | Client Task | | Update Producteev | |

| Date | Details | | Billing | Person |
|---|---|---|---|---|
| ___/___/___ | Client: | | | |
| | | | Tel No | |
| | | | | |
| No Action | | Emailed | | Call Forward | | Client Task | | Update Producteev | |

| Date | Details | | Billing | Person |
|---|---|---|---|---|
| ___/___/___ | Client: | | | |
| | | | Tel No | |
| | | | | |
| No Action | | Emailed | | Call Forward | | Client Task | | Update Producteev | |

| Date | Details | | Billing | Person |
|---|---|---|---|---|
| ___/___/___ | Client: | | | |
| | | | Tel No | |
| | _____ | | | |
| | _____ | | | |
| No Action | | Emailed | | Call Forward | | Client Task | | Update Producteev | |

| Date | Details | | Billing | Person |
|---|---|---|---|---|
| ___/___/___ | Client: | | | |
| | | | Tel No | |
| | _____ | | | |
| | _____ | | | |
| No Action | | Emailed | | Call Forward | | Client Task | | Update Producteev | |

| Date | Details | | Billing | Person |
|---|---|---|---|---|
| ___/___/___ | Client: | | | |
| | | | Tel No | |
| | _____ | | | |
| | _____ | | | |
| No Action | | Emailed | | Call Forward | | Client Task | | Update Producteev | |

| Date | Details | | Billing | Person |
|---|---|---|---|---|
| ___/___/___ | Client: | | | |
| | | | Tel No | |
| | _____ | | | |
| | _____ | | | |
| No Action | | Emailed | | Call Forward | | Client Task | | Update Producteev | |

| Date | Details | | Billing | Person |
|---|---|---|---|---|
| ___/___/___ | Client: | | | |
| | | | Tel No | |
| | | | | |
| No Action | | Emailed | | Call Forward | | Client Task | | Update Producteev | |

| Date | Details | | Billing | Person |
|---|---|---|---|---|
| ___/___/___ | Client: | | | |
| | | | Tel No | |
| | | | | |
| No Action | | Emailed | | Call Forward | | Client Task | | Update Producteev | |

| Date | Details | | Billing | Person |
|---|---|---|---|---|
| ___/___/___ | Client: | | | |
| | | | Tel No | |
| | | | | |
| No Action | | Emailed | | Call Forward | | Client Task | | Update Producteev | |

| Date | Details | | Billing | Person |
|---|---|---|---|---|
| ___/___/___ | Client: | | | |
| | | | Tel No | |
| | | | | |
| No Action | | Emailed | | Call Forward | | Client Task | | Update Producteev | |

| Date | Details | | Billing | Person |
|---|---|---|---|---|
| ___/___/___ | Client: | | | |
| | | | Tel No | |
| | | | | |
| No Action | | Emailed | | Call Forward | | Client Task | | Update Producteev | |

| Date | Details | | Billing | Person |
|---|---|---|---|---|
| ___/___/___ | Client: | | | |
| | | | Tel No | |
| | | | | |
| No Action | | Emailed | | Call Forward | | Client Task | | Update Producteev | |

| Date | Details | | Billing | Person |
|---|---|---|---|---|
| ___/___/___ | Client: | | | |
| | | | Tel No | |
| | | | | |
| No Action | | Emailed | | Call Forward | | Client Task | | Update Producteev | |

| Date | Details | | Billing | Person |
|---|---|---|---|---|
| ___/___/___ | Client: | | | |
| | | | Tel No | |
| | | | | |
| No Action | | Emailed | | Call Forward | | Client Task | | Update Producteev | |

| Date | Details | | Billing | Person |
|---|---|---|---|---|
| ___/___/___ | Client: | | | |
| | | | Tel No | |
| | | | | |
| No Action | | Emailed | | Call Forward | | Client Task | | Update Producteev | |

| Date | Details | | Billing | Person |
|---|---|---|---|---|
| ___/___/___ | Client: | | | |
| | | | Tel No | |
| | | | | |
| No Action | | Emailed | | Call Forward | | Client Task | | Update Producteev | |

| Date | Details | | Billing | Person |
|---|---|---|---|---|
| ___/___/___ | Client: | | | |
| | | | Tel No | |
| | | | | |
| No Action | | Emailed | | Call Forward | | Client Task | | Update Producteev | |

| Date | Details | | Billing | Person |
|---|---|---|---|---|
| ___/___/___ | Client: | | | |
| | | | Tel No | |
| | | | | |
| No Action | | Emailed | | Call Forward | | Client Task | | Update Producteev | |

| Date | Details | | Billing | Person |
|---|---|---|---|---|
| ___/___/___ | Client: | | | |

| | | Tel No | |
|---|---|---|---|

| No Action | | Emailed | | Call Forward | | Client Task | | Update Producteev | |
|---|---|---|---|---|---|---|---|---|---|

| Date | Details | | Billing | Person |
|---|---|---|---|---|
| ___/___/___ | Client: | | | |

| | | Tel No | |
|---|---|---|---|

| No Action | | Emailed | | Call Forward | | Client Task | | Update Producteev | |
|---|---|---|---|---|---|---|---|---|---|

| Date | Details | | Billing | Person |
|---|---|---|---|---|
| ___/___/___ | Client: | | | |

| | | Tel No | |
|---|---|---|---|

| No Action | | Emailed | | Call Forward | | Client Task | | Update Producteev | |
|---|---|---|---|---|---|---|---|---|---|

| Date | Details | | Billing | Person |
|---|---|---|---|---|
| ___/___/___ | Client: | | | |

| | | Tel No | |
|---|---|---|---|

| No Action | | Emailed | | Call Forward | | Client Task | | Update Producteev | |
|---|---|---|---|---|---|---|---|---|---|

| Date | Details | | Billing | Person |
|---|---|---|---|---|
| ___/___/___ | Client: | | | |
| | | | Tel No | |
| | | | | |
| No Action | | Emailed | | Call Forward | | Client Task | | Update Producteev | |

| Date | Details | | Billing | Person |
|---|---|---|---|---|
| ___/___/___ | Client: | | | |
| | | | Tel No | |
| | | | | |
| No Action | | Emailed | | Call Forward | | Client Task | | Update Producteev | |

| Date | Details | | Billing | Person |
|---|---|---|---|---|
| ___/___/___ | Client: | | | |
| | | | Tel No | |
| | | | | |
| No Action | | Emailed | | Call Forward | | Client Task | | Update Producteev | |

| Date | Details | | Billing | Person |
|---|---|---|---|---|
| ___/___/___ | Client: | | | |
| | | | Tel No | |
| | | | | |
| No Action | | Emailed | | Call Forward | | Client Task | | Update Producteev | |

| Date | Details | | Billing | Person |
|---|---|---|---|---|
| ___/___/___ | Client: | | | |
| | | | Tel No | |
| No Action | | Emailed | Call Forward | Client Task | Update Producteev | |

| Date | Details | | Billing | Person |
|---|---|---|---|---|
| ___/___/___ | Client: | | | |
| | | | Tel No | |
| No Action | | Emailed | Call Forward | Client Task | Update Producteev | |

| Date | Details | | Billing | Person |
|---|---|---|---|---|
| ___/___/___ | Client: | | | |
| | | | Tel No | |
| No Action | | Emailed | Call Forward | Client Task | Update Producteev | |

| Date | Details | | Billing | Person |
|---|---|---|---|---|
| ___/___/___ | Client: | | | |
| | | | Tel No | |
| No Action | | Emailed | Call Forward | Client Task | Update Producteev | |

| Date | Details | | Billing | Person |
|---|---|---|---|---|
| ___/___/___ | Client: | | | |
| | | | Tel No | |
| | | | | |
| No Action | | Emailed | | Call Forward | | Client Task | | Update Producteev | |

| Date | Details | | Billing | Person |
|---|---|---|---|---|
| ___/___/___ | Client: | | | |
| | | | Tel No | |
| | | | | |
| No Action | | Emailed | | Call Forward | | Client Task | | Update Producteev | |

| Date | Details | | Billing | Person |
|---|---|---|---|---|
| ___/___/___ | Client: | | | |
| | | | Tel No | |
| | | | | |
| No Action | | Emailed | | Call Forward | | Client Task | | Update Producteev | |

| Date | Details | | Billing | Person |
|---|---|---|---|---|
| ___/___/___ | Client: | | | |
| | | | Tel No | |
| | | | | |
| No Action | | Emailed | | Call Forward | | Client Task | | Update Producteev | |

| Date | Details | | Billing | Person |
|---|---|---|---|---|
| ___/___/___ | Client: | | | |
| | | | Tel No | |
| | _____ | | | |
| | _____ | | | |
| No Action | | Emailed | | Call Forward | | Client Task | | Update Producteev | |

| Date | Details | | Billing | Person |
|---|---|---|---|---|
| ___/___/___ | Client: | | | |
| | | | Tel No | |
| | _____ | | | |
| | _____ | | | |
| No Action | | Emailed | | Call Forward | | Client Task | | Update Producteev | |

| Date | Details | | Billing | Person |
|---|---|---|---|---|
| ___/___/___ | Client: | | | |
| | | | Tel No | |
| | _____ | | | |
| | _____ | | | |
| No Action | | Emailed | | Call Forward | | Client Task | | Update Producteev | |

| Date | Details | | Billing | Person |
|---|---|---|---|---|
| ___/___/___ | Client: | | | |
| | | | Tel No | |
| | _____ | | | |
| | _____ | | | |
| No Action | | Emailed | | Call Forward | | Client Task | | Update Producteev | |

| Date | Details | | Billing | Person |
|---|---|---|---|---|
| __/__/__ | Client: | | | |
| | | | Tel No | |
| | | | | |
| No Action | | Emailed | | Call Forward | | Client Task | | Update Producteev | |

| Date | Details | | Billing | Person |
|---|---|---|---|---|
| __/__/__ | Client: | | | |
| | | | Tel No | |
| | | | | |
| No Action | | Emailed | | Call Forward | | Client Task | | Update Producteev | |

| Date | Details | | Billing | Person |
|---|---|---|---|---|
| __/__/__ | Client: | | | |
| | | | Tel No | |
| | | | | |
| No Action | | Emailed | | Call Forward | | Client Task | | Update Producteev | |

| Date | Details | | Billing | Person |
|---|---|---|---|---|
| __/__/__ | Client: | | | |
| | | | Tel No | |
| | | | | |
| No Action | | Emailed | | Call Forward | | Client Task | | Update Producteev | |

| Date | Details | | Billing | Person |
|---|---|---|---|---|
| __/__/__ | Client: | | | |
| | | | Tel No | |
| | | | | |
| No Action | | Emailed | | Call Forward | | Client Task | | Update Producteev | |

| Date | Details | | Billing | Person |
|---|---|---|---|---|
| __/__/__ | Client: | | | |
| | | | Tel No | |
| | | | | |
| No Action | | Emailed | | Call Forward | | Client Task | | Update Producteev | |

| Date | Details | | Billing | Person |
|---|---|---|---|---|
| __/__/__ | Client: | | | |
| | | | Tel No | |
| | | | | |
| No Action | | Emailed | | Call Forward | | Client Task | | Update Producteev | |

| Date | Details | | Billing | Person |
|---|---|---|---|---|
| __/__/__ | Client: | | | |
| | | | Tel No | |
| | | | | |
| No Action | | Emailed | | Call Forward | | Client Task | | Update Producteev | |

| Date | Details | | Billing | Person |
|---|---|---|---|---|
| ___/___/___ | Client: | | | |
| | | | Tel No | |
| No Action | | Emailed | Call Forward | Client Task | Update Producteev | |

| Date | Details | | Billing | Person |
|---|---|---|---|---|
| ___/___/___ | Client: | | | |
| | | | Tel No | |
| No Action | | Emailed | Call Forward | Client Task | Update Producteev | |

| Date | Details | | Billing | Person |
|---|---|---|---|---|
| ___/___/___ | Client: | | | |
| | | | Tel No | |
| No Action | | Emailed | Call Forward | Client Task | Update Producteev | |

| Date | Details | | Billing | Person |
|---|---|---|---|---|
| ___/___/___ | Client: | | | |
| | | | Tel No | |
| No Action | | Emailed | Call Forward | Client Task | Update Producteev | |

| Date | Details | | | | | | | Billing | Person |
|---|---|---|---|---|---|---|---|---|---|
| ___/___/___ | Client: | | | | | | | | |
| | | | | | | | Tel No | | |
| No Action | | Emailed | | Call Forward | | Client Task | | Update Producteev | |

| Date | Details | | | | | | | Billing | Person |
|---|---|---|---|---|---|---|---|---|---|
| ___/___/___ | Client: | | | | | | | | |
| | | | | | | | Tel No | | |
| No Action | | Emailed | | Call Forward | | Client Task | | Update Producteev | |

| Date | Details | | | | | | | Billing | Person |
|---|---|---|---|---|---|---|---|---|---|
| ___/___/___ | Client: | | | | | | | | |
| | | | | | | | Tel No | | |
| No Action | | Emailed | | Call Forward | | Client Task | | Update Producteev | |

| Date | Details | | | | | | | Billing | Person |
|---|---|---|---|---|---|---|---|---|---|
| ___/___/___ | Client: | | | | | | | | |
| | | | | | | | Tel No | | |
| No Action | | Emailed | | Call Forward | | Client Task | | Update Producteev | |

| Date | Details | | Billing | Person |
|---|---|---|---|---|
| __/__/__ | Client: | | | |
| | | | Tel No | |
| | | | | |

| No Action | | Emailed | | Call Forward | | Client Task | | Update Producteev | |
|---|---|---|---|---|---|---|---|---|---|

| Date | Details | | Billing | Person |
|---|---|---|---|---|
| __/__/__ | Client: | | | |
| | | | Tel No | |
| | | | | |

| No Action | | Emailed | | Call Forward | | Client Task | | Update Producteev | |
|---|---|---|---|---|---|---|---|---|---|

| Date | Details | | Billing | Person |
|---|---|---|---|---|
| __/__/__ | Client: | | | |
| | | | Tel No | |
| | | | | |

| No Action | | Emailed | | Call Forward | | Client Task | | Update Producteev | |
|---|---|---|---|---|---|---|---|---|---|

| Date | Details | | Billing | Person |
|---|---|---|---|---|
| __/__/__ | Client: | | | |
| | | | Tel No | |
| | | | | |

| No Action | | Emailed | | Call Forward | | Client Task | | Update Producteev | |
|---|---|---|---|---|---|---|---|---|---|

| Date | Details | | Billing | Person |
|---|---|---|---|---|
| ___/___/___ | Client: | | | |
| | | Tel No | | |
| | _____ | | | |
| | _____ | | | |
| No Action | | Emailed | | Call Forward | | Client Task | | Update Producteev | |

| Date | Details | | Billing | Person |
|---|---|---|---|---|
| ___/___/___ | Client: | | | |
| | | Tel No | | |
| | _____ | | | |
| | _____ | | | |
| No Action | | Emailed | | Call Forward | | Client Task | | Update Producteev | |

| Date | Details | | Billing | Person |
|---|---|---|---|---|
| ___/___/___ | Client: | | | |
| | | Tel No | | |
| | _____ | | | |
| | _____ | | | |
| No Action | | Emailed | | Call Forward | | Client Task | | Update Producteev | |

| Date | Details | | Billing | Person |
|---|---|---|---|---|
| ___/___/___ | Client: | | | |
| | | Tel No | | |
| | _____ | | | |
| | _____ | | | |
| No Action | | Emailed | | Call Forward | | Client Task | | Update Producteev | |

| Date | Details | | Billing | Person |
|------|---------|--|---------|--------|
| ___/___/___ | Client: | | | |
| | | | Tel No | |
| | | | | |
| No Action | | Emailed | | Call Forward | | Client Task | | Update Producteev | |

| Date | Details | | Billing | Person |
|------|---------|--|---------|--------|
| ___/___/___ | Client: | | | |
| | | | Tel No | |
| | | | | |
| No Action | | Emailed | | Call Forward | | Client Task | | Update Producteev | |

| Date | Details | | Billing | Person |
|------|---------|--|---------|--------|
| ___/___/___ | Client: | | | |
| | | | Tel No | |
| | | | | |
| No Action | | Emailed | | Call Forward | | Client Task | | Update Producteev | |

| Date | Details | | Billing | Person |
|------|---------|--|---------|--------|
| ___/___/___ | Client: | | | |
| | | | Tel No | |
| | | | | |
| No Action | | Emailed | | Call Forward | | Client Task | | Update Producteev | |

| Date | Details | | Billing | Person |
|---|---|---|---|---|
| __/__/__ | Client: | | | |
| | | | Tel No | |
| | | | | |
| No Action | | Emailed | | Call Forward | | Client Task | | Update Producteev | |

| Date | Details | | Billing | Person |
|---|---|---|---|---|
| __/__/__ | Client: | | | |
| | | | Tel No | |
| | | | | |
| No Action | | Emailed | | Call Forward | | Client Task | | Update Producteev | |

| Date | Details | | Billing | Person |
|---|---|---|---|---|
| __/__/__ | Client: | | | |
| | | | Tel No | |
| | | | | |
| No Action | | Emailed | | Call Forward | | Client Task | | Update Producteev | |

| Date | Details | | Billing | Person |
|---|---|---|---|---|
| __/__/__ | Client: | | | |
| | | | Tel No | |
| | | | | |
| No Action | | Emailed | | Call Forward | | Client Task | | Update Producteev | |

| Date | Details | | Billing | Person |
|---|---|---|---|---|
| ___/___/___ | Client: | | | |
| | | | Tel No | |
| | | | | |
| No Action | | Emailed | | Call Forward | | Client Task | | Update Producteev | |

| Date | Details | | Billing | Person |
|---|---|---|---|---|
| ___/___/___ | Client: | | | |
| | | | Tel No | |
| | | | | |
| No Action | | Emailed | | Call Forward | | Client Task | | Update Producteev | |

| Date | Details | | Billing | Person |
|---|---|---|---|---|
| ___/___/___ | Client: | | | |
| | | | Tel No | |
| | | | | |
| No Action | | Emailed | | Call Forward | | Client Task | | Update Producteev | |

| Date | Details | | Billing | Person |
|---|---|---|---|---|
| ___/___/___ | Client: | | | |
| | | | Tel No | |
| | | | | |
| No Action | | Emailed | | Call Forward | | Client Task | | Update Producteev | |

| Date | Details | | Billing | Person |
|---|---|---|---|---|
| __/__/__ | Client: | | | |
| | | | Tel No | |
| | | | | |
| No Action | | Emailed | Call Forward | Client Task | Update Producteev |

| Date | Details | | Billing | Person |
|---|---|---|---|---|
| __/__/__ | Client: | | | |
| | | | Tel No | |
| | | | | |
| No Action | | Emailed | Call Forward | Client Task | Update Producteev |

| Date | Details | | Billing | Person |
|---|---|---|---|---|
| __/__/__ | Client: | | | |
| | | | Tel No | |
| | | | | |
| No Action | | Emailed | Call Forward | Client Task | Update Producteev |

| Date | Details | | Billing | Person |
|---|---|---|---|---|
| __/__/__ | Client: | | | |
| | | | Tel No | |
| | | | | |
| No Action | | Emailed | Call Forward | Client Task | Update Producteev |

| Date | Details | | Billing | Person |
|---|---|---|---|---|
| ___/___/___ | Client: | | | |
| | | Tel No | | |
| | | | | |
| No Action | | Emailed | | Call Forward | | Client Task | | Update Producteev | |

| Date | Details | | Billing | Person |
|---|---|---|---|---|
| ___/___/___ | Client: | | | |
| | | Tel No | | |
| | | | | |
| No Action | | Emailed | | Call Forward | | Client Task | | Update Producteev | |

| Date | Details | | Billing | Person |
|---|---|---|---|---|
| ___/___/___ | Client: | | | |
| | | Tel No | | |
| | | | | |
| No Action | | Emailed | | Call Forward | | Client Task | | Update Producteev | |

| Date | Details | | Billing | Person |
|---|---|---|---|---|
| ___/___/___ | Client: | | | |
| | | Tel No | | |
| | | | | |
| No Action | | Emailed | | Call Forward | | Client Task | | Update Producteev | |

| Date | Details | | Billing | Person |
|---|---|---|---|---|
| __/__/__ | Client: | | | |
| | | | Tel No | |
| | _____ | | | |
| | _____ | | | |
| No Action | | Emailed | | Call Forward | | Client Task | | Update Producteev | |

| Date | Details | | Billing | Person |
|---|---|---|---|---|
| __/__/__ | Client: | | | |
| | | | Tel No | |
| | _____ | | | |
| | _____ | | | |
| No Action | | Emailed | | Call Forward | | Client Task | | Update Producteev | |

| Date | Details | | Billing | Person |
|---|---|---|---|---|
| __/__/__ | Client: | | | |
| | | | Tel No | |
| | _____ | | | |
| | _____ | | | |
| No Action | | Emailed | | Call Forward | | Client Task | | Update Producteev | |

| Date | Details | | Billing | Person |
|---|---|---|---|---|
| __/__/__ | Client: | | | |
| | | | Tel No | |
| | _____ | | | |
| | _____ | | | |
| No Action | | Emailed | | Call Forward | | Client Task | | Update Producteev | |

| Date | Details | | Billing | Person |
|---|---|---|---|---|
| ___/___/___ | Client: | | | |
| | | Tel No | | |
| | _____ | | | |
| | _____ | | | |
| No Action | | Emailed | | Call Forward | | Client Task | | Update Producteev | |

| Date | Details | | Billing | Person |
|---|---|---|---|---|
| ___/___/___ | Client: | | | |
| | | Tel No | | |
| | _____ | | | |
| | _____ | | | |
| No Action | | Emailed | | Call Forward | | Client Task | | Update Producteev | |

| Date | Details | | Billing | Person |
|---|---|---|---|---|
| ___/___/___ | Client: | | | |
| | | Tel No | | |
| | _____ | | | |
| | _____ | | | |
| No Action | | Emailed | | Call Forward | | Client Task | | Update Producteev | |

| Date | Details | | Billing | Person |
|---|---|---|---|---|
| ___/___/___ | Client: | | | |
| | | Tel No | | |
| | _____ | | | |
| | _____ | | | |
| No Action | | Emailed | | Call Forward | | Client Task | | Update Producteev | |

| Date | Details | | Billing | Person |
|---|---|---|---|---|
| ___/___/___ | Client: | | | |
| | | | Tel No | |
| | | | | |
| No Action | | Emailed | | Call Forward | | Client Task | | Update Producteev | |

| Date | Details | | Billing | Person |
|---|---|---|---|---|
| ___/___/___ | Client: | | | |
| | | | Tel No | |
| | | | | |
| No Action | | Emailed | | Call Forward | | Client Task | | Update Producteev | |

| Date | Details | | Billing | Person |
|---|---|---|---|---|
| ___/___/___ | Client: | | | |
| | | | Tel No | |
| | | | | |
| No Action | | Emailed | | Call Forward | | Client Task | | Update Producteev | |

| Date | Details | | Billing | Person |
|---|---|---|---|---|
| ___/___/___ | Client: | | | |
| | | | Tel No | |
| | | | | |
| No Action | | Emailed | | Call Forward | | Client Task | | Update Producteev | |

| Date | Details | | Billing | Person |
|------|---------|---|---------|--------|
| ___/___/___ | Client: | | | |
| | | | Tel No | |
| | _____ | | | |
| | _____ | | | |
| No Action | | Emailed | | Call Forward | | Client Task | | Update Producteev | |

| Date | Details | | Billing | Person |
|------|---------|---|---------|--------|
| ___/___/___ | Client: | | | |
| | | | Tel No | |
| | _____ | | | |
| | _____ | | | |
| No Action | | Emailed | | Call Forward | | Client Task | | Update Producteev | |

| Date | Details | | Billing | Person |
|------|---------|---|---------|--------|
| ___/___/___ | Client: | | | |
| | | | Tel No | |
| | _____ | | | |
| | _____ | | | |
| No Action | | Emailed | | Call Forward | | Client Task | | Update Producteev | |

| Date | Details | | Billing | Person |
|------|---------|---|---------|--------|
| ___/___/___ | Client: | | | |
| | | | Tel No | |
| | _____ | | | |
| | _____ | | | |
| No Action | | Emailed | | Call Forward | | Client Task | | Update Producteev | |

| Date | Details | | Billing | Person |
|------|---------|--|---------|--------|
| ___/___/___ | Client: | | | |
| | | | Tel No | |
| | _____ | | | |
| | _____ | | | |

| No Action | | Emailed | | Call Forward | | Client Task | | Update Producteev | |
|-----------|--|---------|--|--------------|--|-------------|--|-------------------|--|

| Date | Details | | Billing | Person |
|------|---------|--|---------|--------|
| ___/___/___ | Client: | | | |
| | | | Tel No | |
| | _____ | | | |
| | _____ | | | |

| No Action | | Emailed | | Call Forward | | Client Task | | Update Producteev | |
|-----------|--|---------|--|--------------|--|-------------|--|-------------------|--|

| Date | Details | | Billing | Person |
|------|---------|--|---------|--------|
| ___/___/___ | Client: | | | |
| | | | Tel No | |
| | _____ | | | |
| | _____ | | | |

| No Action | | Emailed | | Call Forward | | Client Task | | Update Producteev | |
|-----------|--|---------|--|--------------|--|-------------|--|-------------------|--|

| Date | Details | | Billing | Person |
|------|---------|--|---------|--------|
| ___/___/___ | Client: | | | |
| | | | Tel No | |
| | _____ | | | |
| | _____ | | | |

| No Action | | Emailed | | Call Forward | | Client Task | | Update Producteev | |
|-----------|--|---------|--|--------------|--|-------------|--|-------------------|--|

| Date | Details | | Billing | Person |
|---|---|---|---|---|
| \_\_/\_\_/\_\_ | Client: | | | |
| | | | Tel No | |
| | _____ | | | |
| | _____ | | | |

| No Action | | Emailed | | Call Forward | | Client Task | | Update Producteev | |
|---|---|---|---|---|---|---|---|---|---|

| Date | Details | | Billing | Person |
|---|---|---|---|---|
| \_\_/\_\_/\_\_ | Client: | | | |
| | | | Tel No | |
| | _____ | | | |
| | _____ | | | |

| No Action | | Emailed | | Call Forward | | Client Task | | Update Producteev | |
|---|---|---|---|---|---|---|---|---|---|

| Date | Details | | Billing | Person |
|---|---|---|---|---|
| \_\_/\_\_/\_\_ | Client: | | | |
| | | | Tel No | |
| | _____ | | | |
| | _____ | | | |

| No Action | | Emailed | | Call Forward | | Client Task | | Update Producteev | |
|---|---|---|---|---|---|---|---|---|---|

| Date | Details | | Billing | Person |
|---|---|---|---|---|
| \_\_/\_\_/\_\_ | Client: | | | |
| | | | Tel No | |
| | _____ | | | |
| | _____ | | | |

| No Action | | Emailed | | Call Forward | | Client Task | | Update Producteev | |
|---|---|---|---|---|---|---|---|---|---|

| Date | Details | | Billing | Person |
|---|---|---|---|---|
| __/__/__ | Client: | | | |
| | | | Tel No | |
| | | | | |
| No Action | | Emailed | | Call Forward | | Client Task | | Update Producteev | |

| Date | Details | | Billing | Person |
|---|---|---|---|---|
| __/__/__ | Client: | | | |
| | | | Tel No | |
| | | | | |
| No Action | | Emailed | | Call Forward | | Client Task | | Update Producteev | |

| Date | Details | | Billing | Person |
|---|---|---|---|---|
| __/__/__ | Client: | | | |
| | | | Tel No | |
| | | | | |
| No Action | | Emailed | | Call Forward | | Client Task | | Update Producteev | |

| Date | Details | | Billing | Person |
|---|---|---|---|---|
| __/__/__ | Client: | | | |
| | | | Tel No | |
| | | | | |
| No Action | | Emailed | | Call Forward | | Client Task | | Update Producteev | |

| Date | Details | | Billing | Person |
|---|---|---|---|---|
| __/__/__ | Client: | | | |
| | | | Tel No | |
| | _____ | | | |
| | _____ | | | |
| No Action | | Emailed | | Call Forward | | Client Task | | Update Producteev | |

| Date | Details | | Billing | Person |
|---|---|---|---|---|
| __/__/__ | Client: | | | |
| | | | Tel No | |
| | _____ | | | |
| | _____ | | | |
| No Action | | Emailed | | Call Forward | | Client Task | | Update Producteev | |

| Date | Details | | Billing | Person |
|---|---|---|---|---|
| __/__/__ | Client: | | | |
| | | | Tel No | |
| | _____ | | | |
| | _____ | | | |
| No Action | | Emailed | | Call Forward | | Client Task | | Update Producteev | |

| Date | Details | | Billing | Person |
|---|---|---|---|---|
| __/__/__ | Client: | | | |
| | | | Tel No | |
| | _____ | | | |
| | _____ | | | |
| No Action | | Emailed | | Call Forward | | Client Task | | Update Producteev | |

| Date | Details | | Billing | Person |
|---|---|---|---|---|
| ___/___/___ | Client: | | | |
| | | | Tel No | |
| | _____ | | | |
| | _____ | | | |
| No Action | | Emailed | | Call Forward | | Client Task | | Update Producteev | |

| Date | Details | | Billing | Person |
|---|---|---|---|---|
| ___/___/___ | Client: | | | |
| | | | Tel No | |
| | _____ | | | |
| | _____ | | | |
| No Action | | Emailed | | Call Forward | | Client Task | | Update Producteev | |

| Date | Details | | Billing | Person |
|---|---|---|---|---|
| ___/___/___ | Client: | | | |
| | | | Tel No | |
| | _____ | | | |
| | _____ | | | |
| No Action | | Emailed | | Call Forward | | Client Task | | Update Producteev | |

| Date | Details | | Billing | Person |
|---|---|---|---|---|
| ___/___/___ | Client: | | | |
| | | | Tel No | |
| | _____ | | | |
| | _____ | | | |
| No Action | | Emailed | | Call Forward | | Client Task | | Update Producteev | |

| Date | Details | | Billing | Person |
|---|---|---|---|---|
| ___/___/___ | Client: | | | |
| | | | Tel No | |
| | _____ | | | |
| | _____ | | | |
| No Action | | Emailed | | Call Forward | | Client Task | | Update Producteev | |

| Date | Details | | Billing | Person |
|---|---|---|---|---|
| ___/___/___ | Client: | | | |
| | | | Tel No | |
| | _____ | | | |
| | _____ | | | |
| No Action | | Emailed | | Call Forward | | Client Task | | Update Producteev | |

| Date | Details | | Billing | Person |
|---|---|---|---|---|
| ___/___/___ | Client: | | | |
| | | | Tel No | |
| | _____ | | | |
| | _____ | | | |
| No Action | | Emailed | | Call Forward | | Client Task | | Update Producteev | |

| Date | Details | | Billing | Person |
|---|---|---|---|---|
| ___/___/___ | Client: | | | |
| | | | Tel No | |
| | _____ | | | |
| | _____ | | | |
| No Action | | Emailed | | Call Forward | | Client Task | | Update Producteev | |

| Date | Details | | Billing | Person |
|---|---|---|---|---|
| __/__/__ | Client: | | | |
| | | | Tel No | |
| | | | | |
| No Action | | Emailed | | Call Forward | | Client Task | | Update Producteev | |

| Date | Details | | Billing | Person |
|---|---|---|---|---|
| __/__/__ | Client: | | | |
| | | | Tel No | |
| | | | | |
| No Action | | Emailed | | Call Forward | | Client Task | | Update Producteev | |

| Date | Details | | Billing | Person |
|---|---|---|---|---|
| __/__/__ | Client: | | | |
| | | | Tel No | |
| | | | | |
| No Action | | Emailed | | Call Forward | | Client Task | | Update Producteev | |

| Date | Details | | Billing | Person |
|---|---|---|---|---|
| __/__/__ | Client: | | | |
| | | | Tel No | |
| | | | | |
| No Action | | Emailed | | Call Forward | | Client Task | | Update Producteev | |

| Date | Details | | Billing | Person |
|------|---------|---|---------|--------|
| __/__/__ | Client: | | | |
| | | | Tel No | |
| | | | | |
| No Action | | Emailed | | Call Forward | | Client Task | | Update Producteev | |

| Date | Details | | Billing | Person |
|------|---------|---|---------|--------|
| __/__/__ | Client: | | | |
| | | | Tel No | |
| | | | | |
| No Action | | Emailed | | Call Forward | | Client Task | | Update Producteev | |

| Date | Details | | Billing | Person |
|------|---------|---|---------|--------|
| __/__/__ | Client: | | | |
| | | | Tel No | |
| | | | | |
| No Action | | Emailed | | Call Forward | | Client Task | | Update Producteev | |

| Date | Details | | Billing | Person |
|------|---------|---|---------|--------|
| __/__/__ | Client: | | | |
| | | | Tel No | |
| | | | | |
| No Action | | Emailed | | Call Forward | | Client Task | | Update Producteev | |

| Date | Details | | Billing | Person |
|---|---|---|---|---|
| ___/___/___ | Client: | | | |
| | | | Tel No | |
| | | | | |
| No Action | | Emailed | Call Forward | Client Task | Update Producteev | |

| Date | Details | | Billing | Person |
|---|---|---|---|---|
| ___/___/___ | Client: | | | |
| | | | Tel No | |
| | | | | |
| No Action | | Emailed | Call Forward | Client Task | Update Producteev | |

| Date | Details | | Billing | Person |
|---|---|---|---|---|
| ___/___/___ | Client: | | | |
| | | | Tel No | |
| | | | | |
| No Action | | Emailed | Call Forward | Client Task | Update Producteev | |

| Date | Details | | Billing | Person |
|---|---|---|---|---|
| ___/___/___ | Client: | | | |
| | | | Tel No | |
| | | | | |
| No Action | | Emailed | Call Forward | Client Task | Update Producteev | |

| Date | Details | | Billing | Person |
|---|---|---|---|---|
| \_\_/\_\_/\_\_ | Client: | | | |
| | | | Tel No | |
| | | | | |
| | | | | |
| | | | | |

| No Action | | Emailed | | Call Forward | | Client Task | | Update Producteev | |
|---|---|---|---|---|---|---|---|---|---|

| Date | Details | | Billing | Person |
|---|---|---|---|---|
| \_\_/\_\_/\_\_ | Client: | | | |
| | | | Tel No | |
| | | | | |
| | | | | |
| | | | | |

| No Action | | Emailed | | Call Forward | | Client Task | | Update Producteev | |
|---|---|---|---|---|---|---|---|---|---|

| Date | Details | | Billing | Person |
|---|---|---|---|---|
| \_\_/\_\_/\_\_ | Client: | | | |
| | | | Tel No | |
| | | | | |
| | | | | |
| | | | | |

| No Action | | Emailed | | Call Forward | | Client Task | | Update Producteev | |
|---|---|---|---|---|---|---|---|---|---|

| Date | Details | | Billing | Person |
|---|---|---|---|---|
| \_\_/\_\_/\_\_ | Client: | | | |
| | | | Tel No | |
| | | | | |
| | | | | |
| | | | | |

| No Action | | Emailed | | Call Forward | | Client Task | | Update Producteev | |
|---|---|---|---|---|---|---|---|---|---|

| Date | Details | | Billing | Person |
|---|---|---|---|---|
| __/__/__ | Client: | | | |
| | | | Tel No | |
| No Action | | Emailed | Call Forward | Client Task | Update Producteev |

| Date | Details | | Billing | Person |
|---|---|---|---|---|
| __/__/__ | Client: | | | |
| | | | Tel No | |
| No Action | | Emailed | Call Forward | Client Task | Update Producteev |

| Date | Details | | Billing | Person |
|---|---|---|---|---|
| __/__/__ | Client: | | | |
| | | | Tel No | |
| No Action | | Emailed | Call Forward | Client Task | Update Producteev |

| Date | Details | | Billing | Person |
|---|---|---|---|---|
| __/__/__ | Client: | | | |
| | | | Tel No | |
| No Action | | Emailed | Call Forward | Client Task | Update Producteev |